PRESENTING SOUTH AFRICA

MRS·H·BR33A
MBM 381
BR 75A

PRESENTING SOUTH AFRICA

PETER JOYCE

For Ashley, David and Buzz

Struik Publishers
(A division of New Holland Publishing (South Africa) (Pty) Ltd)
London • Cape Town • Sydney • Auckland

Garfield House
86–88 Edgware Road
London W2 2EA
United Kingdom
www.newhollandpublishing.com

Cornelis Struik House
80 McKenzie Street
Cape Town 8001
South Africa
www.struik.co.za

14 Aquatic Drive
Frenchs Forest
NSW 2086
Australia

218 Lake Road,
Northcote
Auckland
New Zealand

New Holland Publishing is a member of Johnnic Communications Ltd

Please email any comments or updates to: The Editor, Presenting South Africa, updates@struik.co.za

First edition 1998
Second edition 2004

ISBN 1 77007 080 X (9 781770 070806)
10 9 8 7 6 5 4 3 2

Managing editor: Annlerie van Rooyen
Designer: Janice Evans
Design assistant: Lellyn Creamer
Editors: Alfred LeMaitre, Glynne Newlands
Picture researcher: Carmen Swanepoel
Cartographer: Mark Seabrook
Proofreader and indexer: Annelene van der Merwe

Reproduced by Hirt & Carter Cape (Pty) Ltd
Printed and bound by Times Offset (M) Sdn Bhd

PHOTOGRAPHIC CREDITS

CA = Cape Archives; MA = MuseumAfrica; LP = Library of Parliament; SAL = South African Library; IOA = Images Of Africa; WFC = William Fehr Collection, the Castle, Cape Town

Cover: (top left) M Skinner; (top right) J Schadeberg; (middle left) W Knirr/IOA; (middle centre) N Dennis/AfricaImagery.com; (middle right) S Adey/IOA; (bottom left) P Pickford/IOA; (bottom right) MuseumAfrica; **spine**: S Adey/IOA; **back cover**: SAL; **endpapers** (clockwise from top left): G Dreyer/IOA; H von Hörsten/IOA; G Dreyer/IOA; S Adey/IOA; W Knirr/IOA; S Adey/IOA; G Dreyer/IOA; **half title**: R de la Harpe/IOA; **title**: S Adey/IOA; **imprint**: CA/MA; **contents**: H von Hörsten/IOA; **8/9**: WFC; **12**: Adey/IOA; **13** R J Ross/Cape Photo Library; **14/15**: (clockwise from top left): H von Hörsten/IOA;R de la Harpe/IOA; H von Hörsten/IOA; R de la Harpe/IOA; M Lewis/IOA; H von Hörsten/IOA; R de la Harpe/IOA; A Bannister/IOA; **16** (both): State Archives; **17**:R de la Harpe/IOA; **18**: WFC; **20**: MA; **23**: MA; **24**, **25**: Mayibuye Centre; **27**: *The Argus*; **28**: J Schadeberg/ Bailey's African Photo Archives; **29**: E Miller/i-Afrika; **30/31**: MA; **32**: W Knirr/IOA; **35**: W Knirr/; **36**: State Archives; **37**: CA; **38** (all): J Schadeberg; **39**: *The Star*; **40**, **41**:W Knirr; **42/43**: W Knirr/IOA; **44/45**, **46/47**: MA; **48**, **50**: Getaway/D Steele/Photo Access; **50/51**: H Potgieter **51:** A Froneman; **52**: L Stanton; **53**: SAL; **54/55**: H von Hörsten/IOA; **56** (top): CA; **56** (lower): AT Mathews; **58/59**, **60/61**: MA; **62**: W Knirr/IOA; **64**: A Froneman; **65**: MA; **66**: N Dennis/AfricaImagery.com; **67-69**; W Knirr; **70/71** (all), **72**: M Lewis/IOA; **73**: A Froneman; **74/75**: W Knirr; **76/77**: M van Aardt; **78/79**: L von Hörsten/IOA; **80**: W Knirr; **84/85**: LP; **86**: SAL; **87**: R de la Harpe/IOA; **88**: W Knirr/IOA; **90**: Mark van Aardt; **91**: National Parks Board; **92** (top left, bottom left, top right): N Dennis/IOA; **92** (bottom right): L Soule; **93**: N Dennis/IOA; **94**: R de la Harpe/AfricaImagery.com; **95**: L von Hörsten/IOA; **96**, **96/97**: N Dennis/IOA; **98/99**: WFC; **100**: W Knirr/IOA; **102**: MA; **103**: National Archives; **104**, **106/107**: W Knirr/IOA; **108**: AM; **109**: H von Hörsten/IOA; **110/111**: MA; **112**: S Adey/IOA; **114**: MA; **115**: Local History Museum, Durban; **116/117**: H Potgieter; **120**: MA; **121**: R de la Harpe/ IOA; **122**: W Knirr; **123** (both), **124**: R de la Harpe/ IOA; **125**: W Knirr; **126/127**: R Haestier; **128**: R de la Harpe/AfricaImagery.com; **129**: CA; **130**: MA; **131**: R de la Harpe/AfricaImagery.com; **132**: CA; **134**: S Adey/ IOA; **135**: R de la Harpe/AfricaImagery.com; **136**: L Hoffman/IOA; **137** (all): N Dennis/IOA; **138/139**: WFC; **140**: W Knirr; **142**, **143**: H von Hörsten/IOA; **144**: Mayibuye Centre; **144/145**: H Potgieter; **147**: Mayibuye Centre; **148** (top): M Skinner; **148** (lower): H Potgieter; **148/149**: M Skinner; **150**: CA; **151** (all): M Skinner; **152/153**: D Balfour; **155**: MA; **156**: N Dennis/IOA; **157**: W Knirr; **158/159**: LP; **160**: W Knirr; **162** (top left): source unknown; **162** (bottom) De Beers; **163**: MA; **164**: CA; **164/165**: Anglo American Corp; **166/167**: SAL; **168**: LP; **169**: L von Hörsten/IOA; **170**: LP; **171**, **172**: N Dennis/IOA; **173**: N Dennis/AfricaImagery.com; **174**: N Dennis/ IOA; **175**: J&B Photographers; **176**: N Dennis/AfricaImagery.com; **178**: Colour Library/IOA; **178/179**: G Dreyer/IOA; **180/181**: L von Hörsten/IOA; **182/183**: WFC; **184**: S Adey/IOA; **186**: SAL; **187**: CA; **188** (top left): source unknown; **188** (bottom): SAL; **189**: W Knirr/IOA; **190**: source unknown; **191** (all): C Breytenbach; **193**: A Proust/Cape Photo Library; **194**: J Schadeberg; **195**: SAL; **196/197**: D von der Osten/Photo Access; **198**: N Dennis /IOA; **199** (top left): W Knirr; **199** (top right, bottom left and right): L Hoffman /IOA; **200**: S Adey/IOA; **201**: M Skinner; **202/203**: W Knirr; **204**: E Thiel/IOA; **205**: S Adey/IOA; **207**: State Archives; **208/ 209**: S Adey/IOA; **210/211** (all), **214**: G Dreyer/IOA; **215**: W Knirr/IOA; **217**: LP; **218**: S Adey/IOA; **218/219**: H von Hörsten/IOA; **220/221**: G Dreyer/IOA; **222**: J Haigh.

Contents

Introduction

The Land and the Legacy

ZIMBABWE
Musina
SOUTPANSBERG
Limpopo
Makhado
Kruger National Park
LIMPOPO PROVINCE
Polokwane
MOZAMBIQUE
WATERBERG
BOTSWANA
Kgalagadi Transfrontier Park
Lydenburg
Nelspruit
Pilanesberg National Park
Pretoria
Johannesburg
MPUMALANGA
Maputo
Mmabatho
Soweto
Witbank
Mbabane
Molopo
NORTH-WEST
GAUTENG
SWAZILAND
Potchefstroom
Kosi Bay
Sodwana Bay
NAMIBIA
Golden Gate Highlands National Park
Hluhluwe-Imfolozi Park
Vaal
Welkom
Greater St Lucia Wetland Park
Upington
Alexander Bay
Richtersveld National Park
Augrabies Falls National Park
Kimberley
FREE STATE
KWAZULU-NATAL
Gariep
Royal Natal National Park
Tugela
Bloemfontein
Springbok
Maseru
NORTHERN CAPE
Pietermaritzburg
Namaqualand
LESOTHO
Durban
Atlantic Ocean
Gariep
Umzimkulu
SOUTH AFRICA
DRAKENSBERG
Olifants
Great Karoo
Mountain Zebra National Park
EASTERN CAPE
Port St Johns
N
CEDARBERG
Umtata
Clanwilliam
Karoo National Park
Beaufort West
Graaff-Reinet
Great Kei
Great Fish
Sundays
HEX RIVER MTNS
Addo Elephant National Park
East London
West Coast National Park
WESTERN CAPE
Little Karoo
Oudtshoorn
Grahamstown
Robben Island
Paarl
Tsitsikamma National Park
Cape Town
Stellenbosch
George
Knysna
Port Elizabeth
Cape of Good Hope Nature Reserve
Bontebok National Park
Wilderness National Park
Plettenberg Bay
Mossel Bay
Cape Agulhas
Indian Ocean

If one had to choose a single word to describe South Africa, it would be 'diversity'. This is a land of quite remarkable contrasts, evident to even the most casual observer in the splendid variety of its landscapes, in the widely disparate nature of its cities, in the confusion of colours, creeds and cultures that make up its human complement.

Scenically, South Africa could be half a dozen different countries rolled into one. First-time visitors to the Western Cape, for instance, might be surprised and perhaps disappointed when they arrive, for here there are no free-roaming wild animals, no heat-hazed bushveld stretching to far horizons, no safari camps, nothing that speaks of the classic Africa. Instead, they'll see a green and gentle countryside of pastures and vineyards and orchards heavy with fruit, historic homesteads renowned for their elegance, and towns that have matured gracefully over the centuries.

But the Western Cape is a relatively small corner of the wider region, just a section of one of South Africa's nine provinces and quite unlike the other parts. (The nine provincial divisions are Gauteng, North-West, Limpopo Province, Mpumalanga, the Free State, KwaZulu-Natal, the Eastern Cape, the Northern Cape and the Western Cape.) The 'real' Africa is found far to the north-east, on the broad, game-rich savanna plains of Mpumalanga. In between lie the Karoo's sandy, semi-arid flatlands, beyond which is the Highveld, the most prominent segment of the great interior plateau. Loftier and more grandly imposing are the towering heights of the Drakensberg in the east, a range so formidable that just one negotiable pass breaches its main 250-kilometre-long (150 miles) stretch. The eastern coastal belt is subtropically lush, the western a dust-dry, barren wilderness that supports only the hardiest forms of life. Travel far enough west from the rich farmlands of the Pretoria-Rustenburg area, where the maize stands tall and flowers, fruit and fat vegetables are cultivated for the big-city markets, and eventually you reach the red dunes of the Kalahari Desert, where precious little grows. South Africa has been billed as 'a world in one country' – and, clichéd catch-phrase though it is, it does reflect the reality.

Generally speaking, South Africans enjoy a kindly climate, temperate, warm for most of the year, without any oppressive extremes of temperature, the average daily sunshine ranging from 7,5 to 9,4 hours depending on the particular area (as against, say, London's 3,8). Some of the arid western districts get a bare ten or so overcast days in a whole year. The interior plateau, because of its elevation, tends to be cooler than other parts of the world that lie between the same latitudes; the south-western tip of the country, that centring on the city of Cape Town, has a Mediterranean-type climate, the rains more or less limited to the winter months. The eastern regions are almost tropical in their warmth and humidity, and a lot wetter than those of the west.

Because the climate and the soils vary enormously from area to area, nearly every major crop and many minor ones are grown, among them maize (the golden fields take up almost half the arable land), wheat, grain, sorghum, sugar cane, sunflower seeds, tobacco, cotton, deciduous, citrus and subtropical fruits, and grapes both for export and for the Western Cape's flourishing

ABOVE: The Great Karoo – a dry region for most of the year – is briefly and beautifully transformed when the desert flowers bloom. PREVIOUS PAGES: Cape Town's Heerengracht (now Adderley Street), painted by an unknown artist early in the 19th century. PREVIOUS PAGES INSET: Bales of hay decorate the Free State countryside after the harvest.

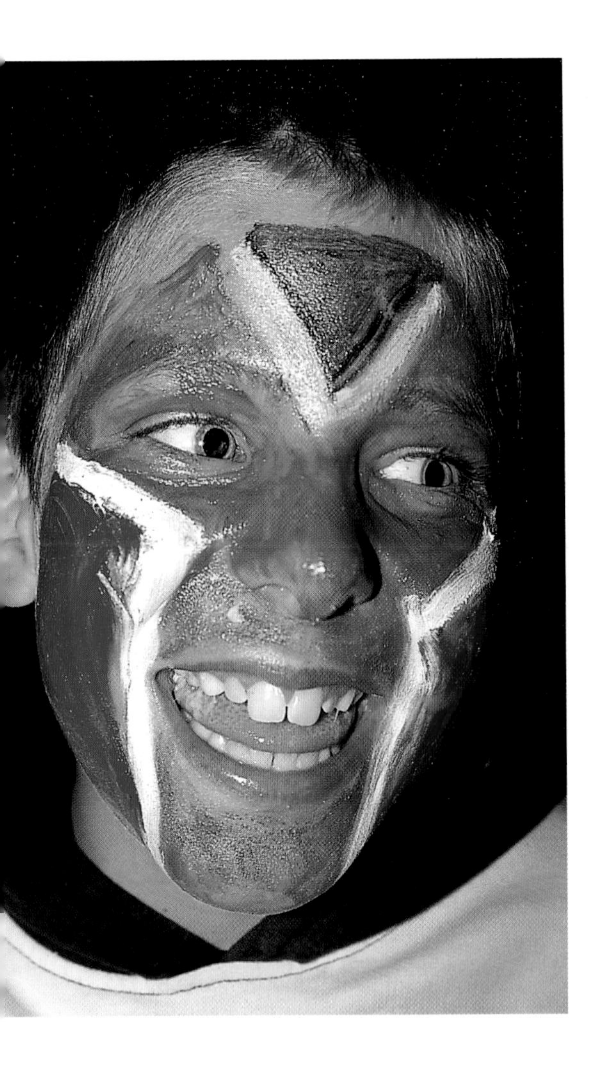

The early 1990s ushered in a new political and social order; national emblems, notably the multihued flag, have helped to bring South Africans closer together.

wine industry. Huge expanses are also given over to livestock: cattle for beef and dairy products; sheep for mutton and wool, goats for meat and mohair; game for venison and hides (the game farms also earn income from tourists). The national wool clip, most of which is produced on the great sunlit spaces of the Karoo and Free State, is the world's fourth largest.

The country is also endowed with exceptional mineral wealth. Beneath its surface lie the earth's largest known reserves of gold, platinum-group metals, high-grade chromium, manganese, vanadium, fluorspar and andalusite, together with vast deposits of cheap coal, uranium, nickel and phosphates. The economy employs advanced technologies; the communications infrastructure is sophisticated; commerce, industry and banking highly developed. In short, South Africa is a regional superpower, accounting for 40 percent of Africa's industrial output, generating 70 percent of its electricity, transporting 75 percent of its railed goods. South Africans drive 46 percent of the continent's motor vehicles and use 36 percent of its telephones.

An impressive litany of assets, it seems. But the figures are deceptive, and when one qualifies them the picture that emerges is a lot less rosy. The comparisons are revealing: the combined southern African region – that embracing South Africa and the neighbouring countries of Botswana, Lesotho, Swaziland, Namibia, Zambia, Zimbabwe, Malawi, Angola and Mozambique – ranks below the tiny city-state of Singapore in terms of trade value; total output of goods and services is on a par with that of Belgium. South Africa itself, with all its agricultural bounty, its mines and industries, has a gross product equal to just that of the American state of Maryland.

It is within these limitations that the country's decision makers must tackle the galaxy of problems, some inherited from the bleakly regressive years of the apartheid era, that belong more to the developing than the developed world: poverty of massive proportions, the social instability that comes with political transition, a cavernous wealth gap between rich and poor, and a desperate need for more jobs, schools, houses, hospitals.

The Rainbow People

The country has an ethnically kaleidoscopic population of some 47 million, the great majority of whom – about three-quarters – are black South Africans. Of these, about half live in the cities and towns, and their number is growing by the year as tens of thousands desert the countryside in search of work and a better way of life. 'Urban drift', in fact, is perhaps the most disruptive, most challenging ingredient of the entire social fabric, because pitifully few of the newcomers manage to find their way into the formal economy. Mass migration is reshaping society, preparing it for the demands of the new millennium, but it is also destroying the traditions, the values, the very character of the old Africa and the cultural identity of its communities.

Despite the process of urbanization and 'detribalization', though, the African people can still be divided by language and custom into distinctive societies. Major groups comprise the Nguni, which embraces the Xhosa of the southern coastal areas and the Zulu and Swazi of the east; the southern and northern Sotho and their cousins the Tswana; the Venda and the Tsonga. All these, in turn, have subgroups, each with its own conventions and convictions, its history and heroes.

Although under sustained assault from Western imperatives, many of the traditional ways survive, relatively uncorrupted, in cultural pockets that have resisted change. Here and there, especially in the remoter villages, you can glimpse the dignified formalities, the subtleties, sounds and strident colours of another place and time. The first new moon of the year heralds the Great Ncwala of the Swazi people (many of whom live in the Mpumalanga province of the north-east), a six-day festival of music, dance, feast, ritual and endurance test that celebrates the rebirth of the chiefs and the first fruits of the earth. Travel through the KwaZulu-Natal country-side and you will occasionally come across beautiful 'beehive' homesteads created by traditional craftsmen, beaded headdresses that denote clan and status, and ceremonial regalia that tells of a long-gone and perhaps prouder age. Venda girls still perform the snake-like *domba* dance to mark their entry into womanhood; Xhosa teenagers smear a whitening clay over their bodies, wear reed costumes and undergo painful circumcision rites as they prepare for adult life; some Ndebele women wear metal rings around ankle, arm and neck and decorate the walls of their homes in bright geometric patterns. And so on: fragments of ancient cultures, the external symbols that have weathered the Western onslaught, are in evidence everywhere. But they are becoming fewer by the year, and what one does see is in many instances especially staged for the visitor.

More durable, though, are the abstract imprints of the different peoples – language and time-honoured folklore; the skills of traditional healing, which co-exist (surprisingly comfortably) with modern medical practice; belief in the presence and authority of the ancestors, and in spirits that inhabit the trees, the rocks and the rivers; customary concepts of wealth and inheritance; the traditional laws of marriage and marital obligation; the sturdy bonds of kinship; the framework of decorum that orders social contact and cements relationships. And then of course there are the crafts and arts themselves: weaving, carving, pottery, poetry and praise-singing, music and dancing.

ABOVE AND OVERLEAF: The many faces of South Africa. Few other nations embrace such a diversity of race, culture, colour, creed and language. Shown above are members of the Western Cape's Coloured community. The following pages show (clockwise from top left) individuals of the Basotho, Xhosa, Cape Malay, Indian, Zulu, Ndebele, Venda and Bushman (or San) communities.

For more than a century – from the time diamonds and gold were found in the northern regions – economic power lay largely in the hands of English-speaking whites, such as the directors of the Consolidated Goldfields Company, shown circa 1895 (top). The land, though, remained with the Afrikaner (above).

This is the village scene, still recognizable as part of Africa as it once was. But some of the legacy, and especially the artistic vibrancy, has been carried into the urban melting pots and there, in the sprawling townships, it is being adapted and developed to produce new forms of expression. Modern South African music is known as *mbaqanga*, an innovative and lively melange of traditional African and Western idioms (American jazz and the big band were major influences), and it is making its mark in the wider world. So too is African drama, or 'black theatre', invariably an exuberant mix of words, dance and song memorable for its freshness and spontaneity.

The far south-west of the country – the Cape Peninsula and its hinterland – is home to most of the country's three million 'Coloured' people. The community has diverse origins, and many of its members are descendants of the slaves brought in from the East by the early white colonists (*see* page 20). Among them are the so-called Cape Malays, an integrated society that has held firmly to its Islamic traditions. The majority of Coloured families, though, are of the Christian faith. South Africa's Indian population numbers about a million, nine-tenths of whom live in and around the Durban area, on the eastern seaboard. Here their forefathers settled, during the later decades of the 19th century, many (initially) as workers on the new and extensive sugar cane plantations of the region (*see* page 115). They too have preserved their heritage: their languages, their religions and the strict codes and disciplines of the patriarchal extended family. White South Africans make up less than a fifth of the country's total population, though for much of the 20th century they have held the reins of political and economic power, relinquishing them only when the post-Cold-War winds of change began to blow away the old alignments. They, too, can be subdivided by language and culture.

The Afrikaners trace their forebears to the Dutch who landed at and colonized the Cape from the early 1650s onwards, and to other white immigrants, notably the French Huguenot (Protestant) refugees who settled part of the hinterland in the 1690s; British (mainly Scottish) Presbyterians; and the Germans who came, in the 19th century, to farm the eastern regions. All these later additions were rapidly assimilated into the main body of Dutch-speaking people, and practically nothing now remains of the various transplanted nationalities that merged into Afrikanerdom. The most discernible of the legacies is perhaps that of the French, who gave their names to many Afrikaans families (Du Toit, Le Roux, Marais, Malan and De Villiers are representative), and their skills to the vineyards and the graceful architecture of the Cape winelands. The Afrikaans language itself stemmed from High Dutch, absorbing new words and idioms from other local communities during three centuries of isolation from Europe.

For much of the colonial period the Afrikaners were a predominantly rural people, their families large and close-knit, semi-nomadic to begin with, bound together by a fierce and sometimes aggressive pride in community and by perceived threats to their national identity. And threats there were: from a Britain bent on conquest and 'anglicization', and from the far more numerous black peoples whose lands they had encroached upon and occupied.

Entirely different in origin and intent were the English-speaking immigrants. They were urban settlers rather than farmer-pioneers. The initial English cultural assault began with the military occupation of the Cape in 1795 (*see* page 20), and was reinforced by periodic migratory waves. Other, much smaller white minorities include those of Portuguese, Greek, German and Dutch stock. The Portuguese, many from the former colonial territories of Angola and Mozambique and from the Atlantic island of Madeira, are estimated to number a substantial 100,000 or so. South Africa's Jewish community, whose roots lie mainly in central and eastern Europe, account for about 2,5 percent of the white population and is strongly represented in the business world and the arts.

First Lords of the Veld

The various groups that now make up the intricate cultural and linguistic tapestry of southern Africa are relative latecomers on the scene. Fully 20,000 years before the first of them arrived, the subcontinent was home to the early Bushmen (also known as San), smallish, lively people who roamed the sunlit plains in freedom, in harmony with themselves and with nature. The Bushmen were hunter-gatherers, Stone Age nomads who went where the seasons led, living off the wild plants of the land and, the southernmost of them, the fruits of the sea.

About 2,000 years ago some of the Bushman groups – those occupying areas of modern Botswana – began to acquire herds of fat-tailed sheep from the Sudanic peoples of the north, so provoking a pastoral revolution that was to have far-reaching consequences. For the first time, the idea of property ownership, and the rights to particular tracts of territory, began to play a part in relationships between the various clans: livestock meant wealth and status, prizes that were worth competing for and fighting over.

The new, more acquisitive, richer folk, known as Khoikhoi (which has been roughly translated as 'men of men') and also, for a time, as Hottentots (a name invented by the early colonists), eventually concentrated in three loose groupings: the Korana in the central regions, around the confluence of the Gariep and Vaal rivers; the Einiqua of the far west, and the Namaqua of the south-west. The last-mentioned, in turn, split into two further groups, one moving up into what is now Namibia, the other filtering down through the coastal strip of Namaqualand to the Cape Peninsula and along the south coast. These were the first indigenous inhabitants to come into contact with the European seafarers.

Meanwhile other peoples, of quite different, iron-using cultures, had settled in the northern subcontinent. They made their appearance as early as AD 250 and belonged to the first migratory wave of Negroid-Hamitic pastoralists, whose ancestral origins lay in the Nilotic north and who are thought to have spoken Bantu languages. The second wave, which began around AD 1100, was much stronger and more sustained. By the 14th century these Bantu-speakers had occupied parts of what is today South Africa's Limpopo Province; 300 years later they were in control of great tracts of the interior and of the eastern seaboard, and their vanguard, the Xhosa, was firmly established in the southern coastal region.

In the course of these great movements of peoples the Bushmen lost their pre-eminent status as lords of the veld. Some of the groups were defeated and destroyed by the more warlike newcomers; others were absorbed into the Bantu-speaking societies (who, among other things,

The wondrous artistic legacy of the Bushmen (or San) is evident in this highly detailed eland and hunter from Kamberg Nature Reserve in KwaZulu-Natal. The nomadic Bushmen built no permanent structures, but they left behind them, on the rocky faces of caves and cliffs, a vividly animated kaleidoscope of paintings and engravings that reveal much about their lifestyle, their mystical beliefs and their gentle, sharing ways.

incorporated some of the Bushman 'click' sounds into their languages). Much later the southern clans came into contact and conflict with the early white settlement at the Cape, and they suffered grievously as a result. Ownership of property was a wholly alien notion to these nomadic folk; cattle were perceived as game, to be killed and eaten when hunger demanded, and their raids on the herds provoked brutal retaliation that occasionally erupted into open warfare, confrontations in which the guns and horses of the settlers usually prevailed. And as the decades passed and the white men expanded and consolidated their hold over the land, large numbers of Bushmen were hunted and killed as 'vermin' (they were more or less officially regarded as such). It appears from some of the records that upwards of 200 000 may have been slaughtered during the first two centuries of colonial occupation.

The Colonial Vanguard

To Renaissance Europeans, Africa was a dark continent indeed, shrouded in mystery and legend, extending southwards beyond the domains of the fabled Prester John to lands inhabited by monsters, a *terra incognita* where men were burned black by the sun and whose desolate shores were lapped by seas that boiled.

For all that, though, it is more than likely that, long before, in classical times, Phoenician seafarers *did* challenge the great unknown to circumnavigate the continent. But the ancient navigational secrets were lost and Africa virtually forgotten during the long, bleak centuries after the disintegration of the Roman Empire. Nor did the later medievals have much incentive to investigate the continent: their traders plied the great overland routes, re-established after the Polo family's epic journeys to China in the 1260s and 1270s, to bring the precious silks and spices from the East. By the early decades of the 15th century, however, the trans-Asian highway was under threat and this, combined with the new spirit of enquiry and adventure that was emerging, prompted Europe's maritime nation-states, and most notably Portugal, to begin exploring Africa's western seaboard and, in time, to seek the sea route to India and the islands beyond.

Diego Cão reached the mouth of the Congo River in 1482 and, on his second voyage three years later, probed down the coast as far as Cape Cross, just north of Swakopmund in today's Namibia. Shortly afterwards Bartholemeu Dias set sail from Lisbon on a 16-month voyage that took his small fleet around Cape Point to Algoa Bay (modern Port Elizabeth) and the mouth of the Great Fish River. A decade later Vasco da Gama sailed past what he called Terro do Natal – he sighted land on Christmas Day 1497 – to Malindi (Kenya) and then, guided by an Arab pilot, crossed the Indian Ocean to Calicut.

Portuguese navigator Bartholemeu Dias erects a *padrão* – an inscribed stone pillar topped by a cross – on the country's southern shores in 1488. Such monuments served as landmarks, as claims to Portuguese sovereignty over new territories, and as expressions of homage to the Christian God.

Yet, although the Portuguese pioneered the trade routes, it was the Dutch who established the first colony on what is today South African soil. In 1652, when Holland's maritime empire was at the height of its power and prosperity, the Dutch East India Company despatched Jan van Riebeeck to the bay that lay beneath Table Mountain, on the south-western tip of the African continent, with orders to 'hastily erect a lodge' for both shelter and defence, and then to build a fort, and to plant a vegetable garden for the replenishment of the passing fleets.

He was also instructed to maintain good relations with the local Khoikhoi, and in this he was only partly successful. The settlers conducted a mutually profitable barter trade with Gogosoa, chief of the main Peninsula groups, but they alienated elements within the Khoikhoi political order. The first 'war', which ended in stalemate, broke out in 1659. Rivalry for the lucrative Dutch connection, and friction between the powerful Cochoqua (who occupied much of the hinterland) and white hunters and farmers, triggered a second confrontation (1673-77).

During their first years on African soil the Dutch made no attempt to create a permanent colony: the settlement was intended simply as a victualling station, useful only for its strategic position at the halfway point between Holland and the Indies. Inevitably, though, it expanded: more Company officials arrived; Van Riebeeck found that he could barely feed his own people let alone the crews of visiting ships, and in due course he turned to private enterprise, releasing a number of men to set themselves up as farmers and tradesmen. There was also something of a labour shortage which, from the later 1650s, he attempted to solve by importing slaves from other parts of Africa and from Madagascar, India and the Malayan archipelago.

These moves had far-reaching consequences. The Cape garrison was now no longer an outpost with limited objectives but a territorial possession capable of growth. It expanded rapidly over the following decades, the area of white settlement spreading northwards and eastwards as the 'freeburghers' – graziers, ranchers, farmers, wine-growers – took over the countryside and displaced the semi-nomadic Khoikhoi. In the east, they eventually came up against the Xhosa. The meeting of two wholly different cultures, competition for grazing land and fear of further white encroachment led to conflict. The first of nine bloody 'frontier wars' erupted in 1779.

By the 1790s Cape Town, the colonial capital, mother city and now widely known as the 'Tavern of the Seas', had grown into a busy seaport town graced by pleasant Cape Dutch-style buildings, the lovely Company Gardens, the Grand Parade, the massive Castle of Good Hope and nascent suburbs that hugged the northern and eastern slopes of Table Mountain. Farther afield, on the banks of the Eerste River to the north-east, lay Stellenbosch, the principal centre of the flourishing wheat, wine and fruit lands. Explorers, missionaries and *trekboers* – semi-nomadic frontier farmers and graziers – had established a tentative settler presence in the great northern interior, and whites were also encroaching in an eastward direction.

All of which seemed satisfactory enough from the colonial perspective, if not from that of the indigenous inhabitants of these regions. But in truth the power of the Netherlands, and the prosperity of the Dutch East India Company, had been in decline since early in the century, a process accelerated by four debilitating Anglo-Dutch wars. British troops landed at and occupied the Cape in 1795, withdrew for a brief period eight years later and returned, to stay, in 1806.

Two and a half millennia ago the Egyptian pharoah Necho is said to have despatched a fleet of sturdy Phoenician biremes down Africa's eastern shores with orders to pass Zanzibar and 'to come back through the Pillars of Hercules [modern Gibraltar] to the Northern Sea and so to Egypt'. The Greek historian Herodotus later recorded that on their return these intrepid seamen swore they had sailed around Libya (the ancient name for Africa) with 'the sun on their right hand'. In other words, the Phoenicians had travelled westwards past what is now the Cape of Good Hope.

Captive slaves on their way into bondage. Cheap labour helped foster an early belief in racial 'superiority', propelling the white colonists onto the long and dangerous road that led to apartheid.

The Racial Divide

Segregation according to race and class had become entrenched during the two centuries of Dutch rule. Slavery erected the first barriers: the rights of men and women forced into servitude were, by definition, severely restricted. By 1795, when British troops first occupied the Cape, the slave population had grown to 17,000, a figure larger than that of the white population. Moreover, the limits of the colony had been relentlessly pushed outwards over a country hitherto occupied by Khoikhoi and Xhosa. By the end of the Dutch era the whites, better organized, better armed and perhaps more tenacious in their quest for the sweet grasses and the good earth, were in control of vast tracts of territory stretching to the Great Fish River in the east and halfway to the Gariep River in the north.

It was during this initial 'pioneering' phase of modern South African history that the pattern of race dominance was established. Whites owned most of the land, and they were in authority militarily, economically and at every level of administration. The status of blacks – Khoikhoi, Bushman, slave, Xhosa and the rapidly growing Coloured population – was largely restricted by law to that of labourer. At that time the great majority of the inhabitants were unskilled and would remain so by official edict. Moreover, social mixing, which was a fairly common and refreshingly civilized feature of the infant Dutch colony, had become a rarity during the latter part of the 18th century, and those who married across the colour line were shunned by 'society'. There was increasing discrimination within the Dutch Reformed Church, the only recognized religious institution, whose congregations had begun to keep separate baptismal records and would later (from about the 1820s) make a practice of holding separate services for whites and blacks. From the 1780s the Cape administration began to introduce indentured and in some instances compulsory labour, together with a 'pass' system that limited freedom of movement.

However, the most significant development of all during the first colonial period was a psychological one. Slavery and a large pool of cheap and (mostly) submissive labour created a general belief among whites that they had been born into a superior race, that menial work was simply not their lot in life, and that a race-based, white-dominated social order was, somehow, God-given. This mentality, bequeathed to succeeding generations, was eventually to lend the force of moral conviction to the creation of the most immoral of societies.

Colonies and Republics

During most of the 19th century a major preoccupation of the colonial regime was the always troubled eastern frontier region. When the British took over in 1806 the Cape's population comprised some 20,000 white settlers, 30,000 slaves and Coloured people, 20,000 Khoikhoi (whose communities had been devastated by smallpox epidemics), scattered groups of Bushmen, and vast but undetermined numbers of Xhosa around and beyond the Great Fish River.

Xhosa and white farmer were at constant odds with each other as the latter continued his eastward infiltration; the most significant of the wars was that of 1819, when the Xhosa army mounted a direct attack on the garrison village of Grahamstown. After bitter fighting this was repulsed, but the incident convinced Somerset that only large-scale immigration could bring a semblance of stability to the region. The decision was translated into action, in the following year, when upwards of 4,000 settlers were brought from Britain to the shores of Algoa Bay and then conducted inland to their allotted farms in the Albany district, the proposed 'buffer zone' between the two racial groups.

Some elements in the colonial government were strongly opposed to military conquest and settler expansion, urging that the borders between black and white territories be fixed and inviolate, that the Xhosa be left in peace to live their lives according to their own customs and laws, and that black-white relationships be stabilized through a series of treaties.

The 'treaty system', which for a while seemed as though it might actually work, was basically a form of what would later become known as 'grand apartheid'. In the nature of the times, though, it was laudable enough. Its intent was at least honest. But eventually the eastward push was resumed, fuelled by territorial greed on the one hand and by the British zeal for 'civilizing', and therefore absorbing, on the other. And the black groups were eventually subdued – inevitably, perhaps, in view of superior white organization and firepower. The process, though, was hastened by one of the most tragic episodes in the country's annals. In 1856-57 the Xhosa deliberately destroyed the greater part of their grain and garden harvests and 200,000 head of their cattle in a massive national sacrifice – a suicidal orgy inspired by the predictions of the prophet Mhlakaza, speaking through his niece Nongqawuse (*see* page 141).

Finally, the regime's frontier policy was reversed yet again, with the passage of the noted Glen Grey Act, which introduced individual land tenure and a modest form of self-government to the territories beyond the Kei River. The Act has been regarded as the first important move to allow black people their basic rights. But it also represented a major and, for the future course of the country's history, highly significant shift in British policy – from a belief that white and black could live together in harmony to the cynical conclusion that they could not, and that 'separate development' offered the only hope for a solution to the race conflict.

In the second decade of the century British colonists also gained a toehold on the far eastern coast. They arrived during what is known as the *Mfecane* (or *Difaqane*), a hugely disruptive series of forced migrations of the black peoples, initially to the west and north of Zululand and eventually over most of the subcontinent. This extraordinary movement had been triggered, largely, by the accession to power, in 1816, of Shaka Zulu: his new and awesomely formidable armies had set out on the bloody path of conquest, igniting a chain reaction of violence and counter-violence as defeated tribes moved on, displacing others, who in turn migrated to spread mayhem in the farther reaches. It was the domino principle in classic and devastating action.

The first Europeans of Natal were members of a party of hunters and traders who arrived in 1824, negotiated a vague land agreement with Shaka and established a settlement at Port Natal, later (in 1834) renamed Durban in honour of the Cape governor of the time. For a brief period (1838-43; *see* page 119) the territory was administered as the Voortrekker republic of Natalia, then it became a British colony governed from Cape Town, receiving its own legislature in 1856. In that year the white population stood at just 8,000, a figure that rose to 60,000 during the next four decades. Whites, though, were always vastly outnumbered by the indigenous Nguni (Zulu) peoples, and were in time to become outnumbered by the Indians, the first of whom arrived in the 1860s as indentured labourers on the great sugar plantations of the coastal regions.

These coastal colonies – the Cape and Natal – were the product of British expansionism. Quite different was the story of white settlement in the great interior.

By the 1830s many of the Cape's Dutch-speaking Boers, and especially those of the outlying areas, were deeply disenchanted with the British colonial government, its authoritarian approach and policies which, though perhaps not liberal in the modern sense of the word, did lay emphasis on racial equality and at times racial assimilation. For these hardy, Calvinistic people, compromise was unthinkable: there was to be no racial parity, no equitable arrangements for the sharing of resources and opportunity and, most certainly, no integration with the indigenous people. After slavery was formally abolished in 1833 (this deprived the Boers of cheap labour), they began moving off in a mass exodus which became known as the Great Trek.

The migration, apparently spontaneous but in fact carefully orchestrated (it was preceded by a number of exploratory expeditions), started in a small way, gathered momentum over the next few years and eventually, when the wanderers became farmers again, succeeded in doubling the area of white settlement in southern Africa.

The story of the Trek is intricate, the broad picture fairly simple. Essentially it had two elements. The first comprised groups of migrants who saw Natal as their promised land and who suffered the massacre of their advance party, led by Piet Retief, in 1837, and then a succession of military reverses, before their laagered discipline overcame a Zulu army at Blood River in December 1838. These eastern trekkers then founded their short-lived republic of Natalia, from which they withdrew, in the face of British military opposition, in 1842.

Some of these Boers returned to the Cape, most rejoined the main body of northern trekkers, the second element, whose ox-wagons had made their way into the lands beyond the Gariep River. These trekkers had already overcome black resistance where this was offered (notably by Mzilikazi's 'raiding kingdom' in a series of fierce battles in 1836; Mzilikazi eventually crossed the Limpopo to found the Ndebele nation of today's Zimbabwe).

By the early 1850s the Boers were numerous enough, and the areas of settlement large enough, to warrant the establishment of two viable independent republics: the Orange Free State (capital: Bloemfontein) between the Gariep and Vaal rivers; and the Transvaal (later known as the South African Republic, or ZAR; capital: Potchefstroom, later moved to Pretoria) between the Vaal and the Limpopo.

Here, there were no liberal sentiments about race. The first Transvaal constitution, promulgated in the mid-1850s, bluntly stated that the settlers 'desire to permit no equality of status between the Coloured people and the white inhabitants'. Nor was there any form of partnership, or 'trusteeship' on the British model, unless it was between master and servant. The concept of dignified coexistence, of defined and protected territories set aside for blacks and within which traditional cultures would be allowed to develop unmolested, was not part of the republican Afrikaner's philosophy at that time.

Boer against Briton

The discovery, in the late 1860s, of huge deposits of diamonds at Kimberley, in the Griqualand West region of the far northern Cape, was a pivotal event: it heralded the industrial age, marking the transformation of southern Africa from a backwater that could safely be ignored to a rich prize in the game of imperial politics.

Of even greater economic and political portent was the immense reef of gold accidentally unearthed, in February 1886, in the Witwatersrand area of the Transvaal, a short distance south of the Boer capital of Pretoria.

Six years earlier Britain and the Transvaal had fought a brief war that had ended in defeat of the former on the slopes of Majuba Hill. The confrontation had little direct connection with diamonds or gold – its roots lay in the British vision of a wider southern African confederation – but it soured relations between the two countries, leaving Britain humiliated and the Boers deeply distrustful of imperial intentions: a distrust that was to prove well founded.

Gold instantly transformed the Transvaal's creaking economy. It also attracted thousands of *uitlanders* (foreigners), most of them English-speaking, to the Witwatersrand, so threatening the Transvaal's Afrikaner identity and, soon enough – because the Uitlander leadership began demanding full political rights – its independence as well. Behind the scenes were schemers with more cynical intent, among them Cecil Rhodes, prime minister of the Cape Colony, empire builder and virtual proprietor of the vast new country of Rhodesia beyond the Limpopo; Joseph Chamberlain, the British colonial secretary, and, from 1897, Alfred Milner, governor of the Cape and high commissioner for South Africa.

Anglo-Boer relations plunged to a new low early in 1896, following the abortive Jameson Raid – an ill-considered and chaotic 'invasion' of the Transvaal led by a small mounted force under the command of the flamboyant Leander Starr Jameson ('Dr Jim'), Rhodes's man in Rhodesia – and continued to deteriorate over the next two years.

The British were determined on the 'unification' of South Africa, a euphemism for bringing the gold-rich Transvaal under their control, by negotiation if possible but by force if necessary. Paul Kruger, the republican president and patriarch of the young Afrikaner nation, tried hard but failed to avoid the final breach ('It is my country you want', he resignedly told Milner) and, on 12 October 1899, after the British had ignored an ultimatum to withdraw their troops from the Transvaal's borders, the guns began firing.

Britain and the European nations expected the Anglo-Boer War to last a few weeks at most, but it took well over two years for the pride of Britain's regiments, more than half a million men in all, to subdue the loosely organized but tenacious mounted commandos of the Transvaal and Orange Free State.

The Anglo-Boer War was a conflict between the whites; the black people had, for the most part, remained on the sidelines, bewildered but stoic in their acceptance of the ravages of war.

Among the bloodiest battles of the Anglo-Boer War was Spioenkop, fought on the Natal front and won, almost by default, by the Boers. Ironically, the objective, a high hill, had practically no strategic value; more than 2,000 troops were killed or wounded in the action. The picture below shows some of the British dead in their trenches.

The Boers won some impressive initial successes (three Imperial armies were defeated in conventional engagements during the disastrous 'British Black Week') and went on to besiege the garrisoned towns of Mafeking, Kimberley and Ladysmith. These were relieved soon enough, and Lord Roberts rolled up the central front to occupy the Boer capitals of Bloemfontein and Pretoria. But the burghers, far from defeat, took to the open veld in highly mobile guerilla units, living off the land and sporadically breaking cover to harrass Kitchener's more numerous, better armed but ponderous forces.

In desperation, Kitchener embarked on a scorched-earth policy; 30,000 homesteads were put to the torch, crops burned, thousands of miles of barbed wire laid, 8,000 blockhouses built to contain the elusive commandos. Farming families, and many of their black workers, were herded into concentration camps in which 26,000 Boer women and children, and an uncounted number of black people, died. Finally, exhausted, the two sides made peace. Its terms, generous to the Boers, were set out in the Treaty of Vereeniging, signed in Pretoria on 31 May 1902, and the respective leaderships began to work together for reconstruction and reconciliation.

An all-white National Convention deliberated the unification of South Africa between October 1908 and May 1909, and on 31 May the following year the four colonies – the Cape and Natal together with the one-time Boer republics of the Orange Free State and Transvaal – became provinces of the Union of South Africa. The form of government chosen was the Westminster model, involving a winner-take-all (almost exclusively white) electoral system, two parliamentary chambers (the senate was a largely advisory forum), four fairly powerful provincial authorities and a governor-general representing the Crown. The constitution was to remain virtually unchanged until South Africa assumed republican status in 1961.

The country's black people had not been consulted during the run-up to Union, and were almost entirely excluded from the new dispensation.

The dictates of apartheid forced tens of thousands of black families off their land. Many were simply dumped in the veld to survive as best they could.

The Seeds of Apartheid

The years between Union in 1910 and the crucial Afrikaner Nationalist electoral victory of 1948 witnessed two world wars, South Africa's transition from a patchwork of largely rural colonies to a relatively powerful industrial nation, and the slow but relentless erosion of what civil rights people of colour had enjoyed under the old regimes.

The country contributed significantly and, in view of the mixed loyalties within its diverse societies

(Afrikaners found it hard to forget the brutalities of the Anglo-Boer War and its concentration camps; blacks had little reason to bless the British), laudably to the Allied effort in both conflicts. Between 1915 and 1918 Union troops conquered German South West Africa (now Namibia), spearheaded the East African campaigns and died in the mud of Flanders fields. During the Second World War (1939-45) they were again prominent in East Africa, and also in the deserts of Egypt and Libya and during the thankless battles of attrition among the hills of Italy.

The two wars, and a world increasingly greedy for raw materials, accelerated an industrial process that had begun with the exploitation of the diamond and gold fields in the later 1800s. This, and the rapid urbanization that came with it, had a far-reaching impact on social patterns, and on race relations. The mines and factories needed labour, so black people had to be brought into the formal economy in large and increasing numbers. At the same time the devastations of the Anglo-Boer War, economic depression and the introduction of modern farming methods were forcing tens of thousands of whites off the land and into the cities, where they found it difficult to adapt to the confined life, often impossible to compete with cheap African labour. The 'poor white' problem, first identified in the 1890s, reached its nadir in the early 1930s.

For decades, black labourers were deemed to be 'temporary' residents of the urban areas; many were housed in soulless hostels with none of the comforts of family life.

Black urbanization went hand in hand with white, and a new proletariat, legally classed as 'temporary', collected in the vast, ramshackle, strictly controlled townships (or 'locations') that began to accumulate around the larger industrial centres (though not, in the beginning, around Cape Town, which from the first years of the 20th century until fairly recently had been regarded as a 'Coloured preference area').

Conflict was endemic to the situation. White wage-earners reacted sharply to the threat; strikes and unrest were regular features of the industrial scene throughout the post-Union period. The most convulsive of the upheavels occurred in 1922, when 22,000 white Rand miners and other workers organized themselves into military-style commandos to confront troops and police in the streets of Johannesburg. Communist elements, curiously, were prominent within the rebel leadership – the uprising was known as the Red Revolt – though how they reconciled egalitarian conviction with anti-black sentiment remains a mystery.

It was in this socio-economic climate that, between the two world wars, successive Union governments expanded the body of race law. Practically nothing had been conceded to African aspirations after the Anglo-Boer War – the British were too intent on a *rapprochement* with Afrikanerdom – and despite strenuous lobbying by a few enlightened Cape leaders, the new Union constitution of 1910 virtually excluded blacks from the political process. Only the 'Coloured vote' in the Cape remained intact (and even this was to be removed, after a series of legislative acrobatics, in the 1950s).

In the two decades that followed Union a whole new arsenal of laws designed to entrench white supremacy and exclusiveness appeared on the statute books. The Mines and Works Act (1911) formalised job reservation; the Natives Land Act (1913) set aside a small portion of the country for black occupation; the Natives (Urban Areas) Act imposed brutal restrictions on the Africans of the towns and cities; and the Immorality Act (1927) prohibited sexual relations between black and white (*see also* below).

Into the Laager

Thus D.F. Malan and the Nationalists of the 1950s and 1960s did not invent apartheid (though they coined the word). What they did do was knit together the existing threads of legal and social prejudice, and create from them one of the most massive and integrated bodies of control legislation ever devised.

Prime architect of the system was Hendrik Verwoerd who, as minister of Native Affairs (1950-58) and latterly as prime minister, helped push through the bedrock Group Areas Act (which divided residential and business areas according to race, and forced thousands of people out of their homes); the Population Registration Act (which classified people according to colour, and from which flowed, among much else, the racially based identity document, a razor-sharp instrument of control and coercion); the Reservation of Separate Amenities Act (which segregated an array of facilities ranging from public buildings and transport to such ordinary community comforts as parks, libraries, beaches, benches and entertainment).

Then there was the appalling Bantu Education Act (1953), aimed chiefly at the thousands of private, mostly church mission schools where, according to a spokesman for the governing party, 'dangerous, liberal ideas are fed by outsiders into untrained minds'. Verwoerd brought black education firmly under State control and reduced its quality in order 'to train and teach people in accordance with their opportunities in life'. These, of course, were largely limited to unskilled and menial jobs.

Verwoerd then went on to lay the foundations of the homelands (Bantustans) structure – the 'Grand Apartheid' design intended to carry segregation to its ultimate, lunatic conclusion. This was based on the assumption that black people had their own, traditional territories where they could and should enjoy citizenship and the vote. Before the end of the apartheid era ten such 'states' had been identified and formalized: Transkei, Ciskei (both in the present Eastern Cape), Venda (Limpopo Province) and Bophuthatswana (scattered over several provinces) were granted full 'independence'; six others achieved semi-independent status.

The Sharpeville massacre, which made headlines around the world, was a turning point in the story of modern South Africa: before the shootings the country, for all the criticism it had attracted, was accepted as a member of the international community; after March 1960 South Africa found itself on a path that led, relentlessly, to total isolation.

Chinks in the Armour

In 1958, on the death of J.G. Strijdom, Verwoerd assumed the premier office to lead the country through some of its most turbulent years, falling victim to a deranged assassin's knife in 1966. Major events during his ruthless stewardship included the Sharpeville massacre (1960), the subsequent banning of the African National Congress (ANC) and other liberation bodies; expulsion from the Commonwealth, and South Africa's transition from dominion to republic (1961).

The massacre at Sharpeville, a township near the Vaal River in what is now southern Gauteng, was especially significant. On 21 March thousands of demonstrators gathered outside the local police station in protest against the hated 'pass laws' (the 'pass' was a reference book, an identity document that was one of the regime's most powerful instruments of control). Reinforcements, including armoured cars, were called in and, when stones were thrown and the crowd pressed forward, the police opened fire, killing 69 people and wounding 186 others.

The Nationalist regime came under increasingly intense pressure, from both internal and external elements, in the 1970s. B.J. Vorster, during his twelve-year tenure (1966-78) as prime minister, had to contend with mounting race conflict at home, though in response to world hostility and the country's creeping isolation from the international mainstream, he did move towards détente, or conciliation, with independent black nations.

P.W. Botha's assumption of office in 1978 coincided with serious regional and internal threats to security in general and to white dominance in particular. The Soweto students' uprising in June 1976 had been an especially traumatic event, setting the pattern – of unrest designed to 'make the country ungovernable' and of violent police reaction – for the future.

Teargas, water cannon, batons and bullets. Behind the unrest of the 1970s and 1980s was a determined drive to 'make the country ungovernable'. The townships bore the brunt of the violence. ABOVE: One of the less traumatic confrontations took place in central Cape Town. The human cost of the campaign was high but, eventually, it brought the apartheid regime to the negotiating table.

Botha's initial response was two-pronged: a tough external policy aimed at destabilizing neighbouring countries through military incursion and support for local resistance movements on the one hand, and a domestic reform initiative on the other. The main thrust of the latter was a new three-chamber constitutional arrangement intended to give Indian and Coloured South Africans a political voice, albeit a limited one. Once again, though, black Africans were excluded from the central process (they were deemed to be citizens of one or another of the ten 'homelands').

The 1984 Botha constitution was roundly condemned by the black opposition; the township troubles escalated; the international community tightened the sanctions screw (the United Nations had declared South Africa a 'threat to world peace' in 1977, imposing the first of the embargoes shortly afterwards) and foreign investors began pulling out in numbers. Clearly, some fundamental decisions had now to be made by the ruling white political establishment.

Voice of the People

The black opposition movement generally and the African National Congress in particular had its origins in the years of disillusionment that followed the Anglo-Boer War. Educated blacks had expected progressive reforms after the two Boer republics had returned to the colonial fold, and were bitterly disappointed when these failed to materialize. The sense of betrayal sharpened after their aspirations were again ignored, by the architects of Union, in 1910, despite repeated representations to the British and South African constitution-makers.

Nevertheless the ANC, formed as the South African Native National Congress in 1912 (it changed its name in 1925), remained committed to peaceful solutions for the next half-century, steadfastly (and perhaps naïvely) holding to liberal expectations over a period during which black rights were progressively eroded.

Nelson Mandela hoisted his colours at the Rivonia trial. 'During my lifetime', he declared, 'I have dedicated myself to this struggle of the African people. I have fought against white domination, and I have fought against black domination. I have cherished the ideal of a democratic and free society in which all persons live together in harmony and with equal opportunities. It is an ideal which I hope to live for and to achieve. But if needs be, it is an ideal for which I am prepared to die.' The words enshrined his vision, defining the principles by which he lived and worked during the long struggle.

In the early 1950s the ANC embarked on a campaign of passsive resistance, affirming that the struggle was not against the white people per se but, rather, against 'unjust laws which keep in perpetual subjection vast sections of the population'. It was a brave effort, but by and large an unsuccessful one. The initial 'defiance campaign' came to an end with the enactment of the draconian Criminal Law Amendment Bill of 1952. Within weeks most of the movement's leadership and a large number of its supporters were in jail. In that year Chief Albert Luthuli, the ANC's president, was awarded the Nobel Peace Prize.

A new initiative began in June 1955, when some 3,000 delegates of all races attended a Congress of the People at Kliptown, near Johannesburg, to endorse the Freedom Charter. This seminal document, heavily socialist in tone, affirmed that South Africa belonged to all its inhabitants and that no government could exercise authority save by the will of the people, and urged the creation of a non-racial democracy. It was the last major attempt at peaceful solutions for more than three decades. Four months later police raided the homes of over 500 activists, the prelude to a massive crackdown that saw thousands arrested, restricted or 'banned'. In December of the following year 156 people were imprisoned preparatory to the most protracted of judicial sagas, the renowned 'treason trial'.

Towards the end of the decade, however, serious divisions began to appear in the ranks of the ANC. The younger, more militant element was fast losing faith in a leadership that rejected violence. Civil disobedience and boycotts had led nowhere; white nationalism was as firmly entrenched as ever. In 1959 the radicals broke away to form the Pan-Africanist Congress (PAC). A year later, following the Sharpeville massacre, both bodies were banned in terms of the Unlawful Organisations Act and went underground.

The nature of the liberation struggle now underwent a fundamental change. The ANC, in collaboration with the South African Communist Party (SACP), with whom it had entered into an alliance, formed its military wing, Umkhonto we Sizwe ('Spear of the Nation'), and launched a wide-ranging campaign of sabotage, initially directed only at 'hard' targets. The government reacted swiftly: some of the organization's leaders, including Oliver Tambo, went into exile; others, among them Nelson Mandela, were arrested.

In 1963, at the conclusion of the celebrated Rivonia trial, Mandela, Walter Sisulu and others were convicted of conspiring to commit nearly 200 acts of sabotage and sentenced to life imprisonment. They were incarcerated on Robben Island, near Cape Town. Mandela remained in prison for the next 27 years, a symbol of defiance, a guiding light for millions aspiring to freedom and, towards the end (and with the help of his fellow-inmates: together they constituted a formidable political forum), the key role-player in the liberation process.

Meanwhile, Tambo's external ANC had been operating with growing effectiveness, making friends in world capitals, establishing a permanent presence – a fully fledged bureaucracy – in London, Dar es Salaam and Lusaka, and developing military camps in Tanzania, Angola and elsewhere. After the 1976 Soweto uprising, and the savage reprisals that accompanied them, these camps accommodated thousands of young refugees from the townships, and from them emerged trained cadres who returned to and waged an underground war within South Africa itself.

LIGHT AT TUNNEL'S END

In January 1989 the ageing P.W. Botha suffered a stroke and relinquished first the leadership of the National Party and then, after a rearguard action against senior colleagues, who argued that the racial divide had to be breached, resigned the presidency in favour of F.W. de Klerk. At the opening of parliament in February 1990, De Klerk lifted the ban on the ANC, the PAC, the SACP and 32 other proscribed organisations, and announced the imminent release of political prisoners. Ten days later Nelson Mandela emerged from his cell to a tumultuous welcome.

The era of white supremacy had come to an end. But it was to be four years before negotiations between 19 widely divergent political bodies produced a democratic South Africa. Notable absentees from the talks were the PAC, which held to its Africanist approach, and Chief Mangosuthu Buthelezi's Inkatha Freedom Party (IFP), which demanded special status for the Zulu nation. The constitutional issues, debated in the Convention for a Democratic South Africa (Codesa), were complex but the main threads plain enough. The ANC wanted a winner-take-all electoral system (simple majority rule) and a unitary state (strong central government); De Klerk's National Party held out for a power-sharing formula that would prevent the 'domination of one group by another' (a euphemism for entrenching white minority rights).

The road to agreement was littered with setbacks. Violence, much of it apparently instigated by a mysterious 'third force', bedevilled the negotiations. Among the excesses were a series of mass killings on suburban trains, the massacre in Boiphatong township, the lethal confrontation between ANC marchers and the Ciskei army in September 1992, and the assassination of Chris Hani, leader of the SACP, in April 1993. Moreover, both the white conservatives, intent on their own *Volkstaat* (people's state), and Buthelezi's Zulu nationalists adopted obstructionist tactics.

Nevertheless a consensus eventually emerged. There was to be a 'government of national unity' in which the major parties would be represented; a parliament of 400 members elected on a system of proportional representation; nine provinces, each with its own assembly, premier and cabinet; a Charter of Fundamental Rights to protect ordinary citizens from unjust action by the State, and a powerful Constitutional Court. These were to be interim arrangements: during the next few years parliament, sitting as a constitutional assembly, would devise a final formula (produced in 1997: it differed marginally from its temporary predecessor).

This was progress indeed. In September 1993 Nelson Mandela called for the lifting of international sanctions; two months later he and De Klerk shared the 1993 Nobel Peace Prize, and the last of the obstacles disappeared in April 1994, just days before the scheduled general election, when Chief Buthelezi agreed to take part in the new order. The ANC gained just less than a two-thirds majority and captured seven of the nine provincial legislatures, losing the Western Cape to the Nationalists (the Coloured vote proved decisive) and KwaZulu-Natal to the IFP.

A month later the world's luminaries gathered at Pretoria's Union Buildings to witness Nelson Mandela's inauguration as the first president of a liberated South Africa. The decades of white supremacy were finally over; the new South Africa had been born, its shape defined by a democratic constitution, its future in the hands of people who had learned, in the hardest of ways, the nature of dignity and the meaning of freedom.

South Africa's first democratic election in 1994 proved something of a revelation: lively, sometimes chaotic but always – incredibly in view of all the enmities of the past – good-humoured.

Nelson Mandela, a free man after nearly three decades in prison, casts his vote in the 1994 election.

CHAPTER ONE

Gauteng

THE GOLDEN HEARTLAND

In his affidavit to the Pretoria Mines Department, prospector George Harrison said: 'I have long experience as an Australian digger,' and then added, in what was perhaps the understatement of the century: 'I think it is a payable gold field.' The date was 24 July 1886.

In the early months of 1886, George Harrison and his friend George Walker, a couple of itinerant and luckless prospectors in need of a job, had agreed to build a house on the farm Langlaagte. One fine February morning they noticed the stones they were unearthing were flecked with yellow. Harrison dug deeper, broke off a piece of conglomerate, crushed and washed it and there, gleaming in the sunlight before him, was a tiny heap of gold. It was a seminal moment: the two drifters had just stumbled on the main reef of the Witwatersrand, the 'ridge of white waters', that was shortly to prove itself the world's most fabulous repository of the precious metal.

Harrison was probably the greatest loser in all of mining history. Unaware of just how momentous his discovery was, he sold his claim for a pitiful £10 and made his way east to Barberton, and into oblivion. Others, though, seized the day. Word of the find spread like the proverbial bushfire and within weeks the bleak, treeless Highveld countryside was dotted with the wagons and bivouacs of the fortune-seekers.

Thereafter Johannesburg grew rapidly, though haphazardly and with practically no thought for the future. In the very early days it was believed that the reef, though rewarding enough for the first syndicates and companies on the scene, was limited in size and, like so many other hoped-for El Dorados, would quickly be worked out. Soon enough, though, richer seams were located and charted; the mines went deeper; gold output, boosted by the new cyanide extraction technique, increased dramatically and the community began to plan for permanence. Conscious of the priorities, it established a stock exchange and racecourse in 1887; a hospital, a school, the Globe Theatre and the renowned Wanderers sporting club made their appearance a year later; and by the early 1890s the 'Randlords' – magnates such as Joseph Robinson, Cecil Rhodes, Barney Barnato, the Wernher family, Solly Joel and Alfred Beit – were creating financial empires that were to become household names.

Today the Johannesburg metropole is Africa's third largest conurbation (after Cairo and Alexandria in Egypt), a vibrant, modern city of gleaming high-rises and traffic-jammed one-way streets, sophisticated shopping malls, exciting nightspots, restaurants that serve exquisite food, galleries, museums (MuseumAfrica is a splendid exposition of the country's cultural heritage) and performing arts venues in which productions – drama, ballet, opera, orchestral music – of international calibre are staged. Nevertheless there are still hints of the old diggers' camp about the place, images evoked by the down-to-earth materialism of its citizens, the urgent pace of their lives and the never-ending quest for quick and easy money. Significantly, Johannesburg's

OPPOSITE PAGE: Johannesburg at night. The city, third largest in Africa, began life when gold was discovered beneath the highveld ground a little more than a century ago. PREVIOUS PAGES: The mining town of Krugersdorp, west of Johannesburg, in the early years of the Witwatersrand. PREVIOUS PAGES INSET: Mine dumps are part of the Johannesburg landscape.

One of the early gold diggers recalled that Johannesburg's best hotel, Heights, 'provided quarters behind walls of metal guaranteed to withstand rain, and was in stupendous demand. The proverbial billiard table gave shelter to sleepers night after night. As for the less pretentious houses, where "rooms" cost anything from £10 nightly – they had the habit of collapsing in rainstorms that pelted the Rand with exceptional heaviness during the first few seasons.'

biggest tourist attraction is Gold Reef City, something like a mini-Disneyland that recreates the life and times of the first rugged inhabitants. The visual legacy is there, too. All around, but especially to the south, are the mine dumps, great mounds of earth and dust that testify to the pre-eminence of gold in the making of Johannesburg. Most of the earlier diggings have long since been worked out, their headgears now rusting quietly in the sun, their dumps clothed in modest coats of greenery, but there is plenty going on farther out, on the East and West Rand.

The inaugural city fathers were not overly concerned with the niceties of urban design. The first town plan was simplicity itself: streets conformed to a strict grid, ignoring the contours of the land; little thought was given to such amenities as gardens, squares and other public comforts, and there are no tree-lined thoroughfares, few open spaces in the central area. Until recently, perfectly functional and in some cases graceful buildings were being pulled down at a frantic rate to make way for newer, shinier, taller structures, and the noise of the jackhammer was a constant refrain – all in the name of progress, of course, and justifiable in economic terms, but the psychology was still that of the brash, pioneering frontier settlement. Today, like so many big cities, the central district is threatened with decay; service industries have relocated to the suburbs, shops have followed in their hundreds, an army of market traders has moved in, and street crime has soared. An ambitious urban renewal scheme is in place, but a lot of money, skill and patience will be needed if the trend is to be reversed.

Inner Johannesburg is South Africa's economic hub, the fast-beating heart of a vast, untidy jumble of mining, industrial and residential satellites, once independent but now part of two great metropoles, or 'unicities', collectively known as the Witwatersrand, or simply as 'The Rand'. To the east are the substantial towns of Benoni (which means 'son of my sorrows': the town was named by an early surveyor frustrated with the site's awkward shape), Boksburg, Germiston (formally proclaimed a city) and Nigel. On the western flank are Carletonville, Westonaria, Randfontein and Krugersdorp. To the south, around the middle reaches of the Vaal River, is another heavily industrialized area, separate from the Witwatersrand though in fact there is not much open countryside between the two. The principal southern centres are Vereeniging and Vanderbijlpark, both attractive enough despite their smokestack status, both born of the Highveld's huge coal deposits and the steelworks they feed.

Less than 60 kilometres (37.5 miles) north of Johannesburg, in the warm valley of the Apies River, lies Pretoria, historic seat of the old Transvaal republican government and now the country's executive capital. It is a handsome metropolis, smaller, rather more sedate than Johannesburg, noted for its stately buildings, its jacaranda trees, its parks and gardens and the wealth of indigenous plant life they sustain. The wider Pretoria municipal area is now known as Tshwane. Between these two heavyweights is Midrand, until quite recently a mere scatter of farmsteads and villages but now a prime growth point, destined to become a city in its own right.

Together, Pretoria, the Witwatersrand and its Vaal River extension occupy more or less the whole of Gauteng, though the sprawling industrial and residential developments are interspersed with swathes of still-rural land given over, for the most part, to farms and smallholdings yielding milk, vegetables, fruit, broiler chickens, eggs and other fresh produce for the vast urban market.

In area, Gauteng is the smallest of South Africa's nine provinces, the most densely populated, and the richest: its 17,000 square kilometres (6,563 square miles), covering just 1.5 percent of the country, is home to around 9 million people (19.7 percent of the total population) who, between them, generate four-tenths of the gross national product. The great majority (nearly nine in 10) are city dwellers, and they are drawn from a kaleidoscopic diversity of cultures and linguistic groups. English, Zulu and Afrikaans are the languages most often heard in workplace and street but others – Sesotho, Tswana, SiSwati, Portuguese, French, Greek, German, Dutch – are also well represented.

Historically, the region has derived by far the greater portion of its wealth from the Witwatersrand's golden treasure house, from the Main Reef that runs some 90 kilometres (55 miles) from Evander in the far east to Randfontein in the west – an impressive distance, but in fact the reef is just a part, a small segment, of the rim of a gigantic gold-bearing 'saucer' that extends deep into the Free State. In the mid-1990s the Witwatersrand section alone sustained 26 large-scale mines together with a number of substantial residue retreatment plants.

The mineworkers, those who go underground, live a hard, dirty and dangerous life. Most of the mines reach enormous depths and the high pressures under which the ore is extracted can trigger what are known as rockbursts, one of the more common causes of fatalities. Gas explosions and rockfalls take their tragic toll; on average, accidents within the gold industry kill around 300 men each year. Many of the seams are narrow, and the shafts (or stopes) are often little more than a metre high. The heat and humidity are intense; rock temperatures can soar to 55°C and, even though refrigerated air is pumped through the ventilation systems, atmospheric conditions can be stifling. Because of the narrowness of the seams, the drilling and blasting processes are still largely manual operations, but new techniques are being developed, and machines are progressively replacing man at the rockface.

The lifeblood of Gauteng: pouring molten gold at a refinery.

The industry, indeed, shed nearly 200,000 jobs in the decade leading up to the mid-1990s, and the down-sizing process continues. Not all the redundancies are due to mechanization: unlike most of the mines elsewhere – in Australia, North America, Russia, and other parts of Africa – none of the gold in the reef lies conveniently close to the surface, and operating at such incredible depths is an expensive business. Production costs increase year by year, outstripping a gold price that is quoted in weakened dollars. Generally, profits have been on a downward trend ever since the commodity began losing its lustre as a hedge against financial uncertainty, and retrenchments steadily add to the already vast army of the unemployed.

There is immense wealth within the borders of Gauteng, but also extreme poverty among the people of the townships and 'squatter camps' that fringe all the major centres. The deprivation, the chasm between rich and poor, coupled with the radical re-ordering of society since the demise of apartheid, has had profound implications for the stability of the region and the peace of mind, the very security, of its residents.

Johannesburg's 'Randlords' spent their wealth freely, ostentatiously, erecting grand homes 'with sky-lights and turrets and scrolled verandahs and gilded tips to their fences'. These palatial pads were built to last; very few have survived the decades.

ABOVE: Early Johannesburg's filigreed elegance. The intricate cast-iron components of this Victorian shopping arcade were prefabricated in and imported from Glasgow in 1893 to serve the wealthier residents of the prosperous mining town. OPPOSITE PAGE: Market Square around the turn of the century.

FACES OF JOHANNESBURG

Nobody pretends that Johannesburg is a beautiful city, but it has its attractions. There is a vibrancy, a bustling, honestly materialistic quality about the place that stimulates the mind, lifts the spirit. And it enjoys a marvellous climate. It lies 1,750 metres (5,740 feet) above sea level on the high central plateau, where the air is rare and heady, the winters clear-skied and not too cold, and where the summer heat is tempered by altitude and (in good years) by brief late-afternoon thunderstorms that often produce cloudbursts of Olympian proportions. On average, the city receives more rain in just four months than England's famously soggy Manchester does in a full year.

The rains wash the dusty earth, greening the grass after the long dry months, bringing an emerald freshness to the gardens and the flowering trees. And there are a great many of the latter, lovely bauhinias and flames, and a score of other species that lend grace to an otherwise rather charmless suburban scene. Greater Johannesburg, in fact, claims to be the most densely wooded of the world's major cities. Unlike the central district, the wider area is unusually well endowed with open space: the metropolitan council and its 'substructures' administer more than 600 different parks, reserves and other public areas.

Suburban Johannesburg is an essay in contrasts. To the north are (to name a few) Houghton, Parktown, Saxonwold, Rosebank and, farther out, Bryanston and Sandton, affluent areas whose dignified, tree-lined avenues gird some of South Africa's most opulent homes. The wealth is discreet, secluded behind high walls and decorous facades, but it is real enough, huge in volume and economic power. Quite different are the inner neighbourhoods and those to the south, most of them rather downmarket, characterless sprawls of modest red-roofed bungalows, unpretentious apartment blocks and shabby commercial streets.

And then there are the townships themselves, populated largely (though by no means exclusively) by the poor. The pattern was set in the very early days. Mine-owners offered work strictly on their own terms: their aim was to make maximum use of the vast reservoir of cheap, unskilled black labour while, on the one hand, parting with as little of their new-found wealth as possible and, on the other, conceding the very minimum in terms of residential and other rights. In line with the conventions and prejudices of the time (and of the almost hundred years that followed), black and white would not be permitted to mix; the two races, although mutually dependent, had to be kept apart at all costs.

The first urban 'location', Pimville, was formally established in 1904, at which time Johannesburg's black population – according to the official figures; the real ones were much higher – stood at 60,000, and over the next seven years it would almost double in size to 112,000 (286,000 in the wider Witwatersrand area). This great labour force was a permanent feature of the new industrial landscape but, still, the authorities deemed it to be 'temporary', regarding its members as migrants, condemning them to a rootless, joyless existence in an urban environment that had no soul and few of the material consolations of life. They were also denied the most basic of civil liberties, reduced to a rock-bottom legal status that was later to be confirmed by a whole arsenal of restrictive statutes beginning with the Natives (Urban Areas) Act of 1923 – which excluded blacks from 'white' land and even from the locations themselves (if, for example, they were felt to be vagrants or 'surplus to labour requirements') – and ending with the Group Areas Act, the Reservation of Separate Amenities Act and other draconian measures pushed through by the 'social engineers' of the 1950s.

These laws allowed officialdom to uproot entire communities and forcibly remove them, out of sight and mind, into the vast, anonymous, ugly dormitory settlements that serve South Africa's urban industrial centres. One such casualty was Cape Town's District Six (*see* page 190); another was Johannesburg's Sophiatown, a dilapidated, crime-ridden, jazz-mad, vital and essentially stable community. Sophiatown, movingly immortalized in Fr Trevor Huddleston's *Naught For Your Comfort*, was demolished and rebuilt as a neat 'white' suburb which, to add insult to grievous injury, was renamed Triomf (Afrikaans for 'Victory').

Largest and best known of Johannesburg's traditionally black satellites is Soweto, a massive conglomerate of what were once 26 separate 'Bantu areas' sprawling over 7,000 hectares (17,300 acres) of dusty veld to the south of the city (the name, in fact, is an acronym for SOuth WEstern TOwnships). The area was consolidated after the Second World War, a

time of rapid industrialization, in what was essentially a slum clearance effort. Some serviced sites were provided; residents were encouraged to erect temporary shelters until more money could be found – which eventually came from an agreement between the Chamber of Mines and Ernest Oppenheimer's giant Anglo American Corporation – and Soweto began to grow. And grow.

Even now, Soweto has few of the amenities that people in the more developed world take for granted – pavements, parks, playgrounds, public pools, libraries, cinemas, theatres and so forth. It is bisected by a single major highway; along either side and stretching to the horizons are row upon dreary row of little square houses lining ill-lit, mostly unpaved and litter-strewn streets. There are no high-rises, few shopping centres. For years, big-business and the retail chain stores ignored the townships, simply because the law forbade them entry, but they are now beginning to move in – which is all to the good, though their arrival threatens the viability of

Snapshots of black life in Johannesburg during the 1950s. BELOW: A family settles in at Orlando Township, early forerunner of Soweto. BOTTOM LEFT: Lost in the township shuffle at a dance-hall. BOTTOM RIGHT: Smoky jam session featuring Jacob 'Mzala' Lepers on bass, Ben 'Gwigwi' Mrwebi on alto sax and Sol 'Beegeepee' Klaaste at the piano.

the thousands of 'spaza' shops (home stores that stock a limited range of highly priced goods) which for decades have served as Soweto's commercial lifeblood. For the rest, much revolves around what is known as the 'informal economy', a term that embraces, among many others, such activities as market trading, home crafts, bricklaying, carpentry, painting, hawking, the shebeen (pub) trade, taxi operations (a highly profitable, competitive and volatile industry) – in fact all those ventures that depend for success on individual enterprise – and, less legimately, prostitution, drug-dealing and car theft.

Soweto has its schools, its university campus, its sports fields and community halls, clinics and hospitals, including the 2,000-bed Chris Hani-Baragwanath. It also accommodates a fast-growing middle class of executives, professionals, entrepreneurs, and a number of its residents are extremely rich, boasting luxurious houses, limousines, servants, bodyguards.

A few have made it against extraordinary odds. As a child, Richard Maponya herded goats on the remote bushveld plains of the present Limpopo Province and then, like so many of his teenage contemporaries, he packed his belongings in a cardboard suitcase and made his way to the big city and, in due course, into the upper echelons of Johannesburg's business community – no mean feat during the era of race discrimination. He started a dairy (without help: the banks refused him loans), built up some capital and branched out into bakeries, liquor outlets and car dealerships. He made millions. In 1997 work began on Soweto's biggest shopping centre, a R570 million development conceived by Maponya and financed and built in 50:50 partnership with one of the big retail chains. Over a third of the shares were offered to and taken up by some 100,000 ordinary Sowetans – which, in his own words, was 'true empowerment of the people who were deprived during apartheid'. In a way, Maponya represents the spirit of Soweto, a place where quick thinking, guts and a willingness to take chances can pay huge dividends.

But Richard Maponya is an unusually gifted man. Few can win as he has done; the majority of his fellow township residents subsist on or not far above the breadline, living half a dozen and more to a room, two to a bed, with even more people – tenants – crowded into a rudimentary shed at the back. The provision of adequate housing is, next to job creation, the biggest challenge of the future, not only here but throughout South Africa.

Soweto comes alive at night and over weekends, the time when folk are free to relax, to take their undemanding pleasures, to gossip about politics and soccer and boxing (the community has produced world champions, legends such as Dingaan Thobela, the 'Rose of Soweto', and the diminutive, lion-hearted Baby Jake Matlala); to drink in and enjoy the music of the shebeens and clubs. There are more than 5,000 of these, ranging from the small, rather basic and marvellously sociable home tavern, where the liquor is cheap and the conversation uninhibited, to the smoothly elegant, subtly lit, collar-and-tie venue offering good music and the finest of vintages.

The music of Soweto is distinctive, full of vitality, but not easily classifiable – its elements and origins are just too diverse. Early township jazz was known as *marabi*, a spontaneous mix of American ragtime and the stamping beat derived from a largely militaristic Zulu heritage (there are relatively few indigenous instruments: much of traditional black South African music is produced by just the drum, the rattle, the voice and the clapping of hands). The first recording

Father Trevor Huddleston

Soweto was originally made up of little more than squatter ghettoes, the homes within them described by a contemporary as 'hovels pieced together with rusty corrugated iron, lengths of hessian, bran and coal bags, boxwood, cardboard and odds and ends ... shin-deep mud in the rainy months, and in winter, incessant screens of blinding dust. Bugs, disease, gangsters ...'.

companies, enticed by an expanding mass urban market, cheap performers and quick profits, exploited *marabi* to the full, demanding and getting, in trumpeter Hugh Masekela's words, 'something to tap your feet to, anything with bounce and rhythm – original or copied, it must sell'. The sounds, though, became more sophisticated as the radio and gramophone introduced the best of African-American jazz and the big-band music of Ellington, Basie and Armstrong.

Meanwhile, other influences were at work, among them the voice-only rural *mbube* of the Zulu 'choral bands', of which Miriam Makeba's 'Wimoweh' is an example; best-known of recent exponents are Ladysmith Black Mambazo of *Graceland* fame. Then there was the joyous *kwela* street music of penny-whistle and homemade guitar, which originated in another Johannesburg township – Alexandra, to the north – and enjoyed enormous popularity between the 1940s and 1960s. Soul music, accompanied by 'soul-dances' (acrobatic routines such as the Monkey Jive) caught on in the 1970s; rock and reggae added more ingredients, and it has all come together under the loose heading of *mbaqanga*. It is a hybrid sound which cannot really be summarized – there are almost as many different styles as there are individual bands – but they all have one thing in common: they are exciting. *Mbaqanga* is the name for African maize bread and, like the food it describes, it fills a void, a deep need.

OPPOSITE: Pretoria's Melrose House, originally the home of a local transport baron. Here, in May 1902, the two warring parties came together to sign the Treaty of Vereeniging, the agreement that finally brought the hugely destructive Anglo-Boer War to an end. BELOW: Pretoria's jacaranda trees in their springtime glory.

CITY OF ROSES

Not long after Pretoria's founding in 1854 as a *kerkplaas*, or 'church place', focal point for *nagmaals* (Calvinist-type communions), baptisms and weddings, it became known as the City of Roses: the climate encouraged luxuriant growth, and in the very early days 'every garden hedge, stoep and even water-furrow' was garlanded by enchanting ramblers. Later came the jacarandas, the first imported at £10 apiece from Rio de Janeiro in 1888. Today 70,000 and more of these exquisite, lilac-blossomed trees grace the parks, gardens and about 700 kilometres (440 miles) of streets. Pretoria is largely an administrative city, home to the political elite and their bureaucrats. But it is also an important communications centre and its advanced industrial complex, based on the huge (though now ailing) Iscor steelworks just outside the city, includes engineering, manufacturing and diamond mining. Just to the east is Cullinan, named after Sir Thomas Cullinan who, in 1905, discovered a fabulously rich kimberlite pipe in the area and developed the Premier Mine, still among the world's foremost diamond workings. In the same year it yielded the famed Cullinan diamond, at 3,016 carats the largest ever unearthed anywhere.

Pretoria, spread out beneath the heights of Meintjieskop, its eastern extremity touching the pleasant foothills of the Magaliesberg, features prominently in the history of Afrikanerdom. This was Paul Kruger's stamping ground, home base to the iron-willed patriarch from 1883 until, with Lord Roberts's columns relentlessly advancing from the south, the old man was forced to flee to Europe and into exile in May 1900. His house still stands, at the western end of Church Street, a surprisingly modest single-storeyed building with a wide verandah on which he held open court, greeting passers-by, receiving his people in informal fashion until the guns of the British drove him away. It now serves as a museum.

Pretoria's Union Building, the inner sanctum of the national government and monument to the unity forged in 1910 between South Africa's English- and Afrikaans-speaking white communities.

The city's hub is Church Square, at the intersection of Paul Kruger and Church streets, an area originally known as Market Square. Here the first place of worship was built, the first open market held and the first shop opened for business. And it could, if the residents had had their way, have become one of the glories of the subcontinent. In the early 1900s many voices were raised in urging the city fathers to create a gracious, spacious piazza of fountains and flowers and Italianate paving, but deaf ears were turned to the pleas and, in 1910, the square was redesigned as a tramway terminus. Still, it has its assets, notably the Old Raadsaal, or republican parliament, completed in 1889 in French Renaissance style with a sprinkling of classical features, and the South African Reserve Bank, designed by the celebrated Herbert Baker.

Pretoria's two most striking architectural legacies, though, come from very different eras, created by people whose dreams for the future were very much at odds with each other – and with those of posterity. Rising grandly from the summit of Meintjieskop is the magnificent,

crescent-shaped Union Building, also the work of Baker and now the administrative headquarters of the national government. It was completed in 1913 to celebrate the coming together of English- and Afrikaans-speaking whites.

South of Pretoria lies the Voortrekker Monument, which commemorates the Great Trek of the 1830s and is regarded by many Afrikaners as a symbol of their national identity. It comprises a monolithic, 40-metre-high (130 feet) block ringed by a 'laager' of 64 granite ox-wagons; inside is the Hall of Heroes, its walls lined by a frieze of marble panels, and a lower chamber that features a granite cenotaph. The latter is so positioned that at precisely noon on 16 December each year – the anniversary of the battle of Blood River, when thousands of Zulu warriors fell to the Boer muskets – a ray of sunshine illuminates the inscription. It is a grand monument, but something of an anomaly in modern South Africa. That it remains open and unblemished speaks volumes for the country's post-apartheid establishment and its generosity of spirit.

'Pretoria is a lovely little spot', wrote Alfred Lord Milner, British high commissioner to South Africa, at the turn of the century, 'of water, trees and gardens, ruined by the most horrible vulgarities of tenth-rate Continental villadom – German architecture of the Bismarckian kind at its worst.' Perhaps this was fair comment at the time. But South Africa's capital had, and in terms of its individual buildings and its hill-girded setting, quite a lot to be proud of. It still has.

The citizens of Pretoria were the first South Africans to set eyes on a motor car, universally hailed as the 'invention of the age': on 4 January 1897 local businessman John Hess (front, second from the right) showed off his Benz Voiturette in the city's Berea Park. His partner A.E. Reno is at the wheel; the passenger is Transvaal state secretary Willem Leyds; Paul Kruger was part of the enthusiastic crowd.

CHAPTER TWO

North-West

REALM OF THE TSWANA

Most of the North-West province's 3.8 million inhabitants – nearly two-thirds of them – are of Tswana stock, a fairly loose cultural and linguistic grouping that embraces the majority of the people of neighbouring Botswana. The Tswana are also historically, and closely, related to the Sotho of the lands to the east and south.

The origins of the Tswana are obscure, shrouded in legends that were born long before the advent of written records. Oral history tells us, however, that the ancestral patriarch was Mogale, a 14th-century chief who ruled the area around the Magaliesberg, or 'Mogale's mountain', a lovely range of hills near Pretoria (*see* page 54). One of Mogale's dynastic successors is thought to have gathered a following and moved westwards, his people eventually splitting up to send out offshoots, some merging with other Sotho-speaking groups, others to remain independent, still others to rejoin the parent body.

This pattern, this dynamic process of fission, migration and fusion, has been a continuing characteristic of Tswana society. Change was constant. The offspring of chiefs did not, as a rule, fight for succession but were inclined rather to break away to form new communities. Yet there were also powerful counter-forces at work, elements that favoured integration, for wealth and status flowed from the ownership of cattle, and the pioneer groups tended to gravitate towards and in many cases allow themselves to be absorbed by those better endowed with livestock.

In neighbouring Botswana, the Tswana's traditional ways are still very much in evidence. The major groupings have retained their separate identities, maintained their ethnic capitals, and still practise a kind of 'village democracy' in which public affairs are debated and disputes settled by the people themselves in conference with their leaders. Much less of the culture, however, has survived across the border in South Africa, where the colonial presence has been heavier and, latterly, far more manipulative. During the 1970s the apartheid regime created an 'independent' homeland for the black people of the region and called it Bophuthatswana, meaning 'that which binds the Tswana'. The country comprised seven small, unconnected chunks of territory, scattered over three of South Africa's four former provincial divisions. Bophuthatswana (now a relatively small part of North-West) was one of four such republics created for the country's major black groups; six others were in the pipeline when apartheid died its unlamented death in 1994.

This exercise in social engineering was a dismal failure. Apart from moral considerations and the political impracticalities, none of the pseudo-states were economically viable. But if any of them could have succeeded it was Bophuthatswana: the land is fertile, much of it turned over to wheat, maize, sunflowers, the remainder to cattle, and beneath the soil, near Rustenburg, there are fabulous deposits of high-grade platinum group metals. The potential was certainly there.

And then there was tourism. Until recently, South African law forbade games of chance (horse-racing, illogically, fell outside the prohibition), but gambling was perfectly legal in the 'homelands', and entrepreneurs were quick to capitalize on the loophole: in 1979 Sol Kerzner,

OPPOSITE PAGE: The turreted opulence of the Palace of the Lost City, the most striking component of the Sun City hotel, entertainment and casino complex. PREVIOUS PAGES: The lovely hills of the Magaliesberg, from an early painting by the artist J.W. George. PREVIOUS PAGES INSET: A king cheetah at Kapama Game Reserve.

BELOW: A carved relief at the Lost City evokes an image of myth and romance. RIGHT: Eland gallop en masse across the dusty veld of the Pilanesberg park, a splendid game sanctuary created next door to Sun City. OPPOSITE PAGE: One of Pilanesberg's rare Cape vultures.

The North-West's premier wildlife success story has been the De Wildt cheetah research centre near Brits. In its first two decades, De Wildt produced more than 400 cheetah cubs, some of which have been released into the wilderness. Moreover, other threatened species, including wild dogs and the rare Cape vulture, have joined the project. Pride of the menagerie, however, is the king cheetah, distinguished from its cousins by its strikingly different markings – the product of genetic variation rather than of an evolving species.

known locally as the Sun King, built the first of his casino-hotel and entertainment complexes in the bleak Bophuthatswana countryside north of the town of Rustenburg. Sun City was the first of several such extravaganzas that made their appearance in the various 'black' territories, and it remained the flagship of the Kerzner fleet, a glittering pleasure-palace of hotels, gaming rooms, sports arena, shops, restaurants, nightclubs, theatres, the world's biggest bingo-hall and a 7,000-seat Superbowl that continues to present the best that international show business has to offer. Forming part of its spacious precincts is the Lost City, centrepiece of which is the sumptuously ornate, columned and turreted Palace Hotel, its fanciful design inspired by some of the grander and less believable myths about the ancient civilizations of Africa. Matching the splendour of Sun City's buildings are the broad acres that surround them, 55,000 hectares (135,937 acres) of beautifully landscaped grounds that embrace, among much else, a 750-metre-long (2,460 feet) man-made lake, swimming pools (including a gigantic one with its own, artificially created surfing waves), waterfalls, streams, lawns, a 'jungle' of 3,500 indigenous trees and two state-of-the-art golf courses.

Sun City is the province's biggest tourism asset. Indeed, it remains the country's foremost inland playground, though with the liberalization of the gambling laws in the later 1990s its premiership is being challenged. More enduring is its near-neighbour, the Pilanesberg park – a magnificent, 60,000-hectare (136,000-acre) expanse of undulating grassland, dense bush and river valley and one of the few southern African reserves that contains a near-complete assembly of the region's original fauna.

The Rich Earth

The province has other sources of wealth, other attractions. To the west of the Johannesburg-Pretoria axis lies the Magaliesberg, a 120-kilometre-long (75 miles) range of hills that, though modest in height and extent, has its beauty and, in the more rugged parts, even its grandeur. The land below lies at a lower altitude than the Witwatersrand to the east; the air is warm and limpid, even in winter; rainfall is relatively high, and a myriad streams and rivulets tumble down the hillsides to feed the earth of the surrounding plains and park-like valleys. The warmth, and the water, create ideal conditions for the growing of peaches and oranges, subtropical fruits, vegetables, cut flowers and much else for the nearby big-city markets and for export.

The Pilanesberg's Nankwe Lake lies at the centre of a series of concentric mountain rings, relics of an aeons-old volcanic convulsion.

The Magaliesberg is one of the last refuges of the Cape vulture, a shy and stately bird that can sometimes be seen wheeling elegantly in the thermals above the hills. The species is now critically rare, for it depends for survival on the bones of animal carcasses crushed to digestible size by the powerful jaws of the hyaena – and hyaenas are now gone from the intensively cultivated lands. The birds have been saved from regional extinction, though, largely by 'vulture restaurants', artificial feeding grounds established in the uplands and, in the breeding season, by their forays into such game-rich areas as the Pilanesberg National Park to the north.

Travel farther westwards, beyond the Magaliesberg and into the wide spaces of what used to be called the Western Transvaal, and you will discover one of the great granaries of Africa – a flattish, golden country of deep soils that, in good times, yields a bounty comparable to those of the world's most productive food-growing regions. Here, there are isolated hamlets that doze their days away in the hot sun, lonely farmsteads shaded by gumtree and emerald willow, pastures that nurture fat cattle, broad fields of wheat, groundnuts, sunflowers, tobacco, citrus and, most especially, of maize. In generous summers, when the rains arrive on time and in quantity, the harvests stretch in fecund luxuriance to the far horizons.

Minerals, too, contribute generously to the North-West's coffers. Indeed, mining accounts for about 55 percent of the province's gross product and employs a quarter of its workforce. Apart from the platinum treasure-trove, the region is also blessed with sizeable deposits of gold, diamonds, high-quality marble, fluorspar (or calcium floride, a mineral which has wide industrial application), iron ore and other commodities.

Solomon Plaatjie, 25 years old at the time of the Mafeking siege, had little formal education but spoke eight languages. He worked in Mafeking as a court interpreter and magistrate's clerk. During the siege he founded the first Tswana-English newspaper – Tsala ea Batho *('Friend of the People') – and later wrote a number of books. Plaatjie was a leader in the black opposition movement, an opponent of the Native Land Act of 1913, and first general secretary of the ANC. He died in 1932.*

MAFEKING: THE MAKING OF A MYTH

Until recently, the capital of the North-West (and of the former Republic of Bophuthatswana) was Mmabatho, which means 'mother of the people' and lies in the dry country of the province's far west, close to the border with Botswana. The name sounds grand enough, but the place barely merited the status of a large town: it embraces little more than the provincial parliament, government buildings, an upmarket hotel, a stadium, a shopping mall and some pleasant residences. Mmabatho, in fact, started life as a suburban appendage of the present provincial capital Mafikeng, a more substantial centre that earned its place in the annals about a century ago. Then known as Mafeking, it served as the administrative hub of the British protectorate of Bechuanaland, and hit the headlines when Boer forces surrounded it during the early days of the Anglo-Boer War.

The siege began on 24 October 1899, lasted 217 days, and turned the garrison's commanding officer, Colonel Robert Baden-Powell, into an instant celebrity. The British public, its patriotic pride dented by a succession of military defeats in the field, was fed a heady diet of jingoistic reports that told of battle, bombardment and bravery, but in reality the siege was an extraordinarily undramatic affair. Baden-Powell, a clever defensive tactician, organized an effective system of trenches, earthworks and dug-out shelters so that everyone, he said, could 'sit tight and wait for them [the Boers] to go'. For the white residents, soldiers and civilians alike, it was

SOLOMON PLAATJIE

FUN & FLY

a tolerable and even enjoyable time – 'like a gigantic picnic', wrote one newspaper correspondent. There were occasional, rather half-hearted raids and counter-raids, and now and again the Boer siege gun, a 94-pound French Creusot artillery piece, would lob a shell into town, but for the most part daily life and the social round went on without interruption. Cricket, polo, pony-racing and football featured regularly on the calendar, though Sunday polo eventually had to be cancelled because Snyman, the religious Boer general, threatened to shell the field. There were theatrical evenings, Sunday concerts, dinner parties. The 'battle' for Mafeking, in short, was something of a myth, though ordinary people in England were led to, indeed wanted to, believe in its heroic quality, and celebrated news of the town's relief with almost orgiastic joy. In due course Baden-Powell was elevated to the peerage and went on to found the Boy Scouts, a movement inspired by the siege (in which he had used young boys as 'runners', or military messengers).

But not everyone in Mafeking had such a good time. The 7,000 Tswana men, women and children suffered grievously: for them, food was in desperately short supply and grew even scarcer when Baden-Powell felt impelled to reduce the grain rations. He also forbade them to buy bread, ordered the execution of a number of them for stealing food, and had many others flogged. Emerson Neilly of the *Pall Mall Gazette* visited their overcrowded and impoverished township, known as the Native Stadt, and confessed that 'words could not portray the scene of misery .... I saw them fall down on the veldt and lie where they had fallen, too weak to go on their way. Hunger had them in its grip, and many were black spectres and living skeletons ...'.

TOP: Some of the defenders of Mafeking; Col. Robert Baden-Powell, garrison commander and, later, founder of the Boy Scout movement, stands at extreme left. ABOVE: A postal service operated during the siege; special stamps were printed. PREVIOUS PAGES: The Hartbeespoort Dam, a prime leisure area, is popular with weekenders from Gauteng.

TOWNS THAT SLEEP IN THE SUN

The North-West has few urban centres of substance. Among the oldest is Potchefstroom, set on the banks of the Mooi River 120 kilometres (75 miles) south-west of Johannesburg and founded in 1838, just after the so-called Nine Days' battle between the Voortrekkers and Mzilikazi's Ndebele. In this confrontation Mzilikazi made use of oxen as cavalry, but despite this imaginative innovation, and despite the boundless courage of his troops, he was forced to concede defeat, and retreated across the Limpopo River into what is now Zimbabwe.

Potchefstroom served as the first capital of the old Transvaal until 1860, when Pretoria was declared the seat of the Boer republican government. However, Potchefstroom has retained much of its early prominence in the culture of Afrikanerdom. The theological college, established soon after the town's founding, has functioned as the Potchefstroom University for Christian Higher Education; its main museum features old weapons, wagons and other artefacts of the trekking years. Other museums also focus on the place's rather serious past, among them

President Pretorius House (the former republican presidential residence) and Totius House, which honours a leading Afrikaans literary figure, Jacob Daniel du Toit.

Klerksdorp, to the west, is a little older than Potchefstroom (it began life in 1837) but its history and character are rather more mundane. Gold was discovered in the area in 1885, provoking a short but dramatic rush for riches: within a year the quiet little village was transformed into a mining camp served by 200 stores, 70 pubs and a stock exchange. The easily accessible gold soon disappeared, however, and so did most of the diggers, but recovery techniques improved over the decades and big companies have moved in to exploit the deeper reserves. Gold is also mined at neighbouring Orkney.

The North-West's only other major industrial town is Brits, towards the eastern end of the Magaliesberg ridge and hub of a region well endowed with mineral resources, including iron ore, chrome, magnesite (used in brick-making) and granite. It also draws prosperity from the subtropical crops grown in the area. Nearby is the acclaimed De Wildt research centre, originally established to breed cheetahs, an enterprise initially dismissed by the sceptics (these endangered carnivores are notoriously difficult to raise in captivity) but which has been a spectacular success.

A conservation scheme of another (though in some respects similar) kind brings interest to the otherwise unremarkable little country town of Lichtenburg, to the north of Potchefstroom. Here the nature reserve, part of the National Zoological Gardens network, serves as an asylum and breeding ground for a variety of rare and exotic animals. Some 35 species are bred and reared in this grassland area, among them pygmy hippo, Indian water buffalo, scimitar oryx and mountain zebra. The Barberspan Nature Reserve, 80 kilometres (50 miles) or so to the south-west, is one of the country's largest and finest waterfowl sanctuaries.

Lichtenburg has other claims to modest distinction. It was the birthplace of Koos de la Rey, arguably the ablest of the Boer commanders during the Anglo-Boer War. And the town, or rather the nearby farm Elandsputte, also provided the setting for the last and perhaps most frenzied of all the great diamond rushes. More than 100,000 diggers congregated on the veld in 1926, just weeks after news of the first find broke; 30,000 of them took part in an officially organized race to peg individual claims, a frantic mass scramble that rivalled anything the American Wild West ever witnessed. Some good stones were found, but the alluvial deposits were soon enough depleted and, by the mid-1930s, Lichtenburg had reverted to its former, much quieter ways.

Lichtenburg is now predominantly a farming centre (it lies at the heart of the so-called 'maize triangle'). So too are Rustenburg and Vryburg, the North-West's two remaining towns of note. Rustenburg, at the western end of the Magaliesberg hills, is now a substantial, pleasantly leafy town, at times even beautiful in its garlands of poinciana and jacaranda and bougainvillea. Tobacco and citrus are two of the region's major crops, though there are many others, the diversity much in evidence in the area's proliferation of nurseries and roadside farmstalls.

Vryburg, focal point of the far-western ranchlands, began life in that especially messy period of colonial expansion when the fringes of white occupation were being pushed north-westwards. In the early 1880s hundreds of Dutch-speaking mercenaries, who had taken part in the wars between the Korana and the Tlhapin peoples, were paid out in a block of land around the

It was at Rustenburg that the quarrelsome mid-19th century Boer leaders came together to patch up their fratricidal differences and end the bitter infighting that was corrupting the first fruits of the Great Trek. The meeting led to the 1852 Sand River Convention which paved the way to full republican status.

Karee-tree mampoer, a powerful alcoholic beverage, was especially loved by Herman Charles Bosman's immortal Oom Schalk Lourens, even though 'it may not be the best kind. Even peach brandy, they say, can make you forget the rust in the corn quicker than the mampoer you make from karee-berries. But karee mampoer is white and soft to look at, and the smoke that rises from it when you pull the cork out of the bottle is pale and rises up in slow curves ...'.

Harts River, which they declared independent. The mini-republic of Stellaland (named after a comet visible in the night skies of the time) lasted just two years, from 1883 to 1885, when a British force was despatched from the Cape to 'remove the fillibusters ... and restore order in the country', but during that time the Stellalanders managed to lay out their capital Vryburg ('free town'), design and fly a flag, issue postage stamps that are now valuable collector's items, and build a much-needed gaol, the ruins of which can still be seen. The latter proved especially useful in the succeeding years, when cattle and horse rustlers roamed the largely lawless land.

About 90 kilometres (55 miles) west of Rustenburg lies Groot Marico, set in the lush valley of that name and enshrined in South Africa's annals by the genius of Herman Charles Bosman. The author of mostly humorous stories, Bosman was a profoundly complex character, eccentric,

impetuous by nature, highly original in thought, contrary in all things. 'He searched', wrote a contemporary, 'for purity in filth and, like [Oscar] Wilde, found stars in the gutter.' At the age of 21 he was arrested for and convicted of killing his stepbrother, condemned to death, and eventually reprieved. He later wrote of his prison experiences, not without hilarity, in *Cold Stone Jug*, but he is best remembered for the time he spent in Groot Marico. It was here, among the lucerne and maize fields, the tobacco lands and citrus groves that the simple, earthy characters of *Mafeking Road* and *Jurie Steyn's Post Office* played their whimsical parts, speaking in English but conveying the very essence of Afrikaans. This is a part of the country long renowned for the quality of its mampoer, a powerful home-distilled brandy-type liquor. Vistors can explore the area, most enjoyably, along the officially sanctioned 'mampoer route'.

One of the last and liveliest of the great diamond rushes took place at Lichtenburg in 1926, when upwards of 30,000 men raced across the flat veld to peg their claims.

CHAPTER THREE

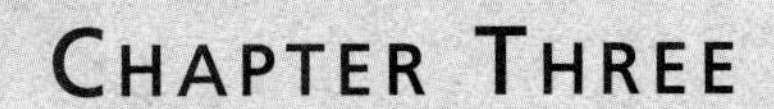

Limpopo Province

BEYOND THE LINE OF CAPRICORN

The hill-clad, wooded country to the north of Tzaneen, where giant and ancient cycads grow and villagers still follow the ways of their forefathers, is the realm of the Rain Queen. She is also known as Modjadji, which means Ruler of the Day, and as Khifidola-maru-a-Daja, the Transformer of Clouds.

The original Modjadji, it is believed, was a 16th-century princess of the Karangan empire in what is now Zimbabwe, granddaughter of the mighty Monomotapa himself. When accusations of incest were levelled against her she fled south, making her way across the Limpopo River, taking with her the rain-making magic and the sacred beads. In due course her descendants became rulers of the Lobedu people, mysterious royal personages who were respected, even feared throughout southern Africa. Shaka himself, the great warrior-king of the Zulu, held the Queen in awe.

There is still a Rain Queen – the title is ritualistically and mystically handed down through the generations – though perhaps the image is more romantic than the reality. She lives a secluded life in her royal residence on the slopes of a gentle hill, close by a great forest of cycads, and she may be visited by a favoured few. When drought settles over the land many of the local folk, white farmers among them, plead for her intercession.

Poverty and Riches

The Lobedu belong to the Northern Sotho cultural group which, during the apartheid years, was consigned to a 'homeland', or 'national state', called Lebowa, in today's Limpopo Province. The territory comprised a scatter of six entirely separate areas which, together, covered a modest 2 million hectares (almost 5 million acres) of generally dry bushveld countryside that sustains cattle, sheep, goats, subsistence and cash crops. Lebowa, though, was never a viable economic unit: most of its people remained poverty-stricken; the richest of them were those who found jobs in the mines and industries of the Witwatersrand.

Indeed, the Limpopo Province is among the poorest of South Africa's nine political divisions. Its five million or so inhabitants account for nearly 12 percent of the national population but the gross regional product comes in at little more than three percent of the total. Per capita income is by far the lowest in the country; unemployment is at a critically high level. On the other hand the province has its natural assets, its economic potential. What it desperately needs are the means – the infrastructure, investment capital and, above all, the skills – to exploit its fallow wealth.

The region is relatively well endowed with minerals, among them copper, coal, platinum and iron ore. Agriculture and ranching, though, remain the backbone of the economy: the great bushveld spaces are ideal for herds of cattle; maize, sunflowers, cotton, groundnuts and table

OPPOSITE PAGE: Wild azaleas decorate the countryside around Haenertsburg, near Tzaneen. PREVIOUS PAGES: An early view of the Limpopo River, the province's northern border. PREVIOUS PAGES INSET: Part of a decorated wall in the land of the Venda.

ABOVE: The impala lily brings splashes of brightness to the often dry, dun-coloured bushveld. OPPOSITE PAGE: Mat-makers display their wares at Elim mission station near Makhado Town in the early 20th century. Limpopo Province is among the country's poorest regions; crafts and one-man businesses play a vital part in the local economy.

grapes flourish in the central areas; the deep soils farther to the east sustain fine orchards of tropical fruits, tea and coffee plantations and, among the hills around Tzaneen and Makhado (formerly Louis Trichardt) Town, massive man-made forests. To the east of Mokopane (Potgietersrus) are the citrus estates of Zebediela, among Africa's most extensive: they support well over half a million trees which, between them, produce some 500 million oranges each year. At harvest time – the Valencias ripen between August and October; the navels from April to June – the groves are laden with fruit and the air is heady with their scent.

And then there is tourism, or, more specifically, ecotourism. Slicing across the province, from the Polokwane (Pietersburg) area in the east to Thabazimbi in the west, is the Waterberg range of hills. They are modest in height, but beautiful in parts, well watered by perennial streams, and they have given their name to the 16,000-square-kilometre (6,187-square mile) expanse of bush terrain that sprawls north to the Limpopo River. This was once big-game country: before the white farmers and ranchers moved in, from about the mid-19th century, it supported vast numbers of antelope, giraffe, zebra, wildebeest. Human settlement depleted, almost extinguished the herds, but some of the larger properties have been retained as private game areas, and although most of them are perhaps less pristine in character than those of Mpumalanga (*see* page 91), they rank among the more rewarding of the country's game-viewing destinations.

The wider region's biggest and best-known tourism asset is the Kruger National Park – or rather, a little more than half the park: the provincial boundary cuts through this most splendid of sanctuaries, the southern segment falling within Mpumalanga (*see* page 91). Limpopo Province, though, probably has the better bargain. Its portion, which runs northwards from the Olifants River, is wilder, less commercially developed than the grasslands of the south, its wide spaces covered by the butterfly-leafed mopane tree, by bushwillow and, along the streams that slice through the area, by strips of dense riverine vegetation, all of which combine to support a huge proliferation of life forms. Largest of its rest-camps are Olifants, magnificently set on cliffs that rise 100 metres (330 feet) and more above the watercourse of that name; Letaba, sited on a sweeping bend of the Letaba River; and Shingwedzi, an atmospheric, somewhat old-fashioned place notable for its spacious grounds, its handsome acacias and palms, and its bright pink-and-white impala lilies. However, Punda Maria, named after the wife of an early ranger, is arguably the most inviting of the venues: it is in the far north, smallish, unpretentious, popular for its sociability and colonial-type charm, and for its setting among rocky hills and groves of evergreen trees.

In contrast to some of the southern camps, Punda Maria has a distinctive and evocative wilderness feel about it. The impression is well founded: this is a unique and, in geophysical terms, quite extraordinary region, the meeting place of fully nine of Africa's major ecosystems. The landscapes are remarkable in their variety, the marvellous mix embracing bushveld and grassland, woodland and dense forest, sandveld, wetland, lava flat, granite hill, high ridge, deep valley and dramatic gorge – a kaleidoscopic environmental mix complemented by an incredible diversity of plant and animal life. Some of the species are tropical, others are found only in this particular area. Especially impressive are the massive Lebombo ironwoods, the mahoganies and ebonies, the groves of ghostly fever trees standing pale in the hushed jungles of the Luvuvhu's river banks, the giant and primeval baobabs of the Mashikiri plateau, and the prolific game of the Hlamalala plain, known as 'South Africa's Serengeti'.

The Great North Road

The highway that runs 530 kilometres (330 miles) north from Pretoria to the great, grey-green Limpopo River – greater perhaps in Kiplingesque legend than in reality – is wide, straight and, in its first stretch, that which leads to the Waterberg, scenically rather featureless. Beyond, though, the countryside becomes more varied, lusher, even tropical. Indeed, just to the north of Polokwane you cross the line of Capricorn, and towards the end of the route are the grand hills of the Soutpansberg. The highway is known as the Great North Road, and it was born in the high summer of Empire, when men like Cecil Rhodes in southern Africa and Horatio Herbert Kitchener, satrap of Egypt and the Sudan, dreamed of and schemed for a direct line of communication between Cape Town and Cairo, and of a continental map painted a bright Imperial crimson. Today it serves less ambitious purposes.

Polokwane is the largest town along the way. It is also the provincial capital, once a bastion of conservative Afrikanerdom and now the seat of a colour-blind provincial legislature. It is a pleasant, rather unpretentious city but one with all the amenities that go with its official

It was in the Waterberg region that the mystic genius of Eugéne Marais, the great naturalist, achieved its most enduring expression. Marais, a man of many parts – lawyer, journalist, innovative writer, poet, medical student, classical scholar and passionate Afrikaner nationalist – retreated into isolation in the early 1920s to ponder the mysteries of nature and to refine his vision. Here he produced two works that were, much later, to gain international acclaim: The Soul of the White Ant *and* My Friends the Baboons. *But the bright flame was soon extinguished: he had suffered recurrent bouts of malaria and painful neuritis, for which he took morphine. His dependence on drugs and alcohol, and his deep fits of depression, led to a tragic death: on 29 March 1936 he committed suicide.*

status, well laid out, its long main street ending with some panache in an open-air gallery of modern and highly original sculptures. The local nature reserve is an attractive, fairly large expanse of golden grassland, acacia bush, rock outcrop and, in wintertime, the vivid blood-red and orange of aloe. A short distance to the south is the Bakoni Malapa 'living museum' of traditional North Sotho buildings, in and around which skilled craftsmen work in the ways of their ancestors. Here you can view the making of pots and baskets, beer and maize meal.

Mokopane, just down the road, also has its nature reserve, though a somewhat ususual one. Part of the National Zoological Gardens network, it serves as one of the country's two animal breeding centres, numbering among its residents such oddities as the pygmy hippo (from West Africa); the Madagascan lemur; the capybara, largest of the world's rodents (it hails from the central Amazon region); the South American llama, the hog deer (from Asia), and others. For a long time the centre's main motivation was the preservation of endangered exotic species but the emphasis is changing, and the place is now home to some of southern Africa's own threatened wildlife – the cheetah, the black rhino, the bushbuck, the roan antelope and so on. Other, less vulnerable animals can be seen in the adjacent bushveld reserve.

Much of the famed Kruger National Park falls within the province's boundaries – a slice of the 'real' Africa that attracts thousands of foreign visitors. BELOW: Elephants on the move. OPPOSITE PAGE: A baobab tree etched against the day's last light.

The town formerly known as Potgietersrus was founded in 1858 and named after Boer commandant Hermanus Potgieter, who had been killed four years previously. The incident and its sequel rank among the most infamous in the annals of colonial occupation in southern Africa. Tension between the local Ndebele and the Boers had been rising ever since the latter began arriving in the area in numbers, much of the hostility triggered by the white farmers' demand for cheap labour and the forays they mounted in quest of young slaves – or rather, since slavery had been outlawed, for 'apprentices'. The most energetic of the slave-raiders was Potgieter, a cold-blooded bully feared throughout the region. His principal victims were the people of Chief Mokopane.

Matters came to a head in 1854 when there was an uprising of sorts and 42 whites were killed (Potgieter among them) in four separate engagements, after which Mokopane led his 2,000-strong community into the safety of a large cave complex. A powerful Boer commando, though, soon located the communal refuge, and for a month the two sides exchanged sporadic gunfire. Then an eerie silence fell upon the day, and when the Boers cautiously made their way forward they saw, in the flickering light of their torches, the corpses of hundreds of Ndebele. Altogether, about a thousand had died in the cave, most of them from thirst; of the remainder, many were shot as they tried to surrender; others (mainly women and children) were taken captive. A horrific episode, one that shows how bitterly black and white competed for the far northern region, and that the Great Trek, long touted by official sources as a peaceful migration into 'empty' territory, was as much about conquest as settlement.

Several other places, smaller and for the most part attractive country towns, line the Great North Road at intervals. Southernmost is Bela-Bela (Warmbaths), named for its refreshing mineral springs, centrepiece of a major health resort. Well to the north is Makhado, originally christened Louis Trichardt after the ill-fated Voortrekker leader and set beneath the misty, wooded Soutpansberg range of hills. Directly overlooking the town is a peak called Hanglip, clothed in a beautiful forest reserve and the burial ground of the Venda chieftains of old.

Last of the centres is Musina (Messina), in a mineral-rich area (the location of South Africa's largest copper mine) close to the Beit Bridge that crosses the Limpopo River into Zimbabwe. Musina is almost entirely surrounded by a forest reserve created to protect the bushveld's ancient baobabs. Other tree species here number a remarkable 350 or so, some of them still waiting to be identified. Within the reserve, too, are outcrops of Sand River Gneiss, rock strata formed 3.8 billion years ago, and among the world's most ancient geological formations.

The tranquillity of rural Venda. These proud people are thought to have originated, at least in part, in the great Karangan empire of what is today Zimbabwe.

Venda and Ndebele

The higher slopes of the Soutpansberg are green, lush, cool, well watered by perennial streams – altogether, an enchanting part of the country, visually appealing, tranquil. Not nearly so peaceful, though, is its history. The area was settled by the Venda, a proud, culturally distinct people who remained firmly in control of the land until the very end of the 19th century – despite the arrival of the better armed Boers five decades before.

The Venda are something of a mystery, perhaps because not all share a common ancestry. The majority of the early arrivals are believed to have originated in the Great Lakes region of East Africa, progressing in slow migratory waves southwards to and through what is now Zimbabwe. Some may have crossed the Limpopo as far back as the 12th century; others stayed on within and as an integral part of the mighty Karangan empire, sharing in its power and prosperity, before they too moved on. These were the Makhwinde of the Rozvi group, who brought with them some of the ingredients of the Great Zimbabwean culture, including the distinctive stone enclosures that dot the countryside. They also imposed their unifying authority on the resident clans of this part of the Limpopo Province. History reveals them as tough, independent-minded folk, well able to resist the incursions not only of the Boers but of the Pedi, Swazi and Tsonga as well.

Venda girls perform the sinuous *domba*, or python dance, to celebrate their entry into womanhood.

For a few years during the later apartheid era the Venda lived within their own national borders: their 'historic homeland' was the smallest of the four 'independent republics' (it extended over just 16,834 square kilometres [6,500 square miles] and supported a population of around half a million). Despite its modest size, though, the region is remarkable both for the variety and beauty of its landscapes and for the complex beliefs and folklore of its people. Perhaps the most striking of its physical features is Lake Fundudzi, South Africa's largest natural expanse of fresh water though, technically, not a proper lake but rather the product of an ancient and massive landslide. The lake is part of the old Africa, and it is sacred to the vhaVenda. Mysterious, too, is the Holy Forest, a dense expanse of indigenous woodland which has served as a sacrosanct burial place and which outsiders may look at but not explore.

Other traditional 'homelands' within Limpopo are the Gazankulu and KwaNdebele regions, both of which enjoyed semi-independent status as part of Pretoria's 'grand apartheid' design. Gazankulu, in the eastern part of the province, was deemed to be the historic land of the Shangaan-Tsonga people. The group moved into the area in 1895, but had in fact taken on a collective identity long before, during the first years of the Zulu empire. Soshangane, one of Shaka's ablest generals, fled north shortly before 1820 to establish his own kingdom among the Tsonga of Gazaland (part of today's Mozambique), but after a clash with Portuguese colonists recrossed the border into an area that now fringes the Kruger National Park.

KwaNdebele, as its name suggests, was home to a section of the Ndebele, a small enclave carved out of the bushveld plains some way to the north-east of Pretoria. These people, too, are of Nguni stock, many of them descendants of those who joined Mzilikazi on his odyssey through the northern interior (*see* page 129). Of the two Ndebele groups, the northern one has lost most of its Nguni heritage: its members have been assimilated by the Sotho, whose language they speak. The southern group, on the other hand, has remained culturally distinct; many of its

Ndebele rural art is widely known for its bright originality. Some of the homesteads are rectangular affairs, thatched, attractively gabled and pedimented, and the walls of the surrounding courtyards are strikingly decorated in eye-catching geometrical patterns. Initially, natural ochres provided the browns, yellows and pinks; lime and soot the whites and blacks. The first designs were simple triangles, V-shaped motifs and parallel lines; later, stylized representations of recognizable objects – plants, animals and so on – were introduced and then, with urbanization and the advent of synthetic paints, the range broadened to include city scenes, buildings and other modern subjects. There is nothing particularly significant in terms of religion, folklore or myth about this unusual art form: the pictures are painted by the women of the household simply to please the eye.

Many of the rural Ndebele women still favour traditional clothing and ornamentation; intricate beadwork is a striking feature of the style.

womenfolk – those who have remained wedded to the rural life – still favour traditional costume. The style is both unique and colourful, comprising beaded blankets and aprons and heavy metal rings around ankle, wrist and neck.

East to the Great Letaba

The road from Polokwane east to Tzaneen is just under 100 kilometres (62 miles) long, and it passes through some of the province's most pleasant countryside. It is especially attractive around Haenertsburg, a village renowned for its azaleas and cherry blossoms. This is the edge of the northern plateau; the route then winds up the lower slopes of the Magoebaskloof.

The uplands here are truly lovely. Most of the higher ground is the domain of the Forestry Department, and much of it is under plantation, but there are also dense glades of natural forest to delight the senses. Perhaps the most enchanting patch is the Woodbush, home to magnificent redwoods, yellowwoods, giant ironwoods, cabbage trees and red stinkwoods. A place for walking, and for communing with the restful spirits in the quietness beneath the deep-green canopy. Around the turn of the century John Buchan, teller of stirring tales, maintained a simple hideaway shack close to the Magoebaskloof. Forty years later, he recalled with nostalgia: 'Two pictures I have always carried to cheer me in dismal places,' he wrote. 'One is of a baking noon on the highveld. The other is the Wood Bush in the Northern Transvaal .... You climb to it through the bare foothills, and then suddenly you cross a ridge and enter a garden. The Wood Bush itself is the extreme of richness and beauty. The wind blows as clear as in mid-ocean ...'.

Among the wooded hills not too far away are the Debegeni Falls, entrancing in the surge and clarity of their waters. To the south lies George's Valley, named after a road engineer with poetry in his heart: he fell in love with the vistas and made gratuitous detours so that travellers could enjoy the finest of them. Here, too, is the dense mantle of the New Agatha forest. Farther south still is the Wolkberg Wilderness Area, nearly 18,000 hectares (44,488 acres) in extent and a place of peak and ravine, thick forest, tumbling stream and waterfall. The area, 2,050 metres (6,725 feet) above sea level at its highest point, supports only a modest game complement – the larger animals were shot out by the growers of illicit cannabis, free spirits who hid in the valleys and lived off the land – but it is still sanctuary for the black eagle and other raptors.

The wider area's main town is Tzaneen, which started life (in 1903) as an experimental station for tropical and subtropical food plants, later serving as base for Dr David Annecke's research into malaria. His work eventually led to the virtual eradication of the disease from the region (though some especially hardy strains have recently re-emerged), enabling the commercial farmers to move in and prosper. The town lies in the immensely fertile Letaba River valley; the soils are rich, the rains usually generous; great plantations of tea mantle the countryside and the air, in the long harvesting months from September through to May, is fragrant with the scent of the fresh leaves. Not just tea, though: the valley sustains citrus and bananas, avocado pears, mangoes, pawpaws, litchis, passion fruit, guavas, tomatoes, winter vegetables, pecan and macadamia nuts, and cotton. Pine forests cover the hillsides, and flowering trees are everywhere.

The Wolkberg is home to the solitary, strange-looking hamerkop, known to rural folk as the 'bird of doom' and usually seen standing motionless in shallow water. To disturb it, some say, will bring disaster. Its nest is an extraordinary affair, an enormous domed structure of grass, mud and bits of rubbish, slowly built over a period of up to six months and often a co-operative effort between three or four of the birds.

LEFT: Darkness slips quietly over the waters of the Tzaneen Dam. The surrounding uplands are clothed in deep-green pine trees. PREVIOUS PAGES: Tea plantations mantle the fertile hillsides near Tzaneen.

Chapter Four

Mpumalanga

Mountain and Lowveld

Mpumalanga's prime and most durable assets remain its scenic splendours and the magnificence of its wildlife heritage. Tourism has long been a big money-spinner and, providing development is handled with sensitivity, will prove the saving grace of a region struggling to contrive a better quality of life for all its people.

*M*ake your way to the top of South Africa's north-eastern Escarpment, to World's End on the rim of Blyde River Canyon, and the vistas that unfold will long remain in the memory. The red sandstone faces of the massive gorge fall away from the heights, steeply and in places precipitously, to the waters of the Motlatse River far, far below. Towering above the chasm is an awesome bevy of buttresses, among them Sundial Peak and the Three Rondavels – hump-like features that vaguely resemble the homesteads traditional to some rural societies – and Mariepskop, a craggy massif named after a hero of the Pulana people who, long ago, resolutely defended his craggy domain against an invading Swazi army. Beyond, to the east, is the low, flat, heat-hazed bushveld plain that stretches across Mozambique to the Indian Ocean.

The Blyde River Canyon ranks among the great wonders of Africa and is arguably Mpumalanga's most eye-catching physical feature. But it is by no means the only natural showplace in a region blessed with quite spectacular scenic variety and splendour.

The Highveld Plateau

The Escarpment, prominent though it is, accounts for a relatively small slice of Mpumalanga's 82,000 square kilometres (31,661 square miles). Nearly three-quarters of the province is occupied by the plateau grasslands of the Highveld and Middleveld that sprawl away to the east of Gauteng – a countryside of open, undulating, rather bland terrain that for the most part and for much of the year is dry, dusty, drably tinted in shades of ochre and brown. But in summer, if the rains are good, the land is transformed, its pastures and broad acres of maize, sorghum and sunflowers combining to create a rich tapestry of greens and golds. Autumn can also delight the eye: March and April bring out the cosmos, an invasive weed (from Mexico) but a beautiful one nevertheless, its white, pink and lilac flowers conferring a profusion of delicate colour on roadside, hill, valley and cultivated field.

There is richness, too, beneath the soil. Nearly half of South Africa's estimated 115 billion tons of coal (58 billion of which are workable at current technological levels; the reserves are the largest in the southern hemisphere) are located on Mpumalanga's plateau, much of it beneath the flattish, scenically rather unremarkable countryside not far from the Gauteng border.

The seams are especially thick and accessible around the town of Witbank, sustaining more than twenty collieries that, together, earn the country a sizeable chunk of its foreign currency inflow each year. They also feed the vast Sasol liquid fuel plants at Secunda, to the south, and the

Opposite page: The great Blyde River Canyon, among South Africa's most celebrated natural wonders. 'Blyde' means 'joy' in Afrikaans, a reference to a happy reunion of eastward-trekking Boers in 1840. Previous pages: Near Pretoriuskop in the southern part of the Kruger National Park. Previous pages inset: One of the Kruger National Park's chacma baboons.

three biggest of the several coal-fired power stations that generate 70 percent of South Africa's electricity. Middelburg, close to Witbank and one of several urban centres that reinforce the economic muscle of this, the industrial western segment of the province, is also a coal-mining centre but its preoccupations are wider, embracing agriculture, communications (it is an important rail hub), steel, vanadium and a proliferation of lesser manufacturing enterprises.

These places have few claims to beauty: they exist largely if not exclusively to create material wealth, and the mines, generating plants, power lines and factories disfigure (and pollute) what was once a pleasant landscape. Each, though, has its own personality and its modest attractions and, for all its industrialization, large parts of the land remain surprisingly unspoilt. Drive a short distance north from Middelburg, for instance, and you will encounter a different world. Here, Loskop Dam captures the flow of the Olifants River, creating a spacious expanse of limpid water that serves as something of a mecca for anglers in quest of the lake's fat carp, kurper and yellowfish, for picnickers, yachtsmen and watersports enthusiasts.

Farther east, beyond the smokestack belt, are other substantial plateau centres, solid and unpretentious country towns that draw their prosperity not from the minerals of the earth but from its benevolent soils. Standerton and Bethal are sustained by the maize, sunflower seeds, groundnuts and, especially, by the dairy products of the surrounding farms. The land around Ermelo, a pleasantly tree-lined place with a fine civic centre, yields these commodities and more, including wool, timber and coal (it is the country's principal source of anthracite). It is also noted for the myriad aquatic birds of Lake Chrissie, the largest natural expanse of fresh water in South Africa, and for the sturdy little Basuto-type ponies bred in the area. Piet Retief, on the edge of the Highveld to the south-east, named after a Voortrekker folk hero (*see* page 119) and once capital of what must have been the modern world's smallest independent territory (its white settlers, all 72 of them, elected a 'president' and claimed such status in the late 1800s), counts paper mills, sugar plantations, tropical fruit orchards and tobacco fields among its assets.

All of which suggests that this is a flourishing region, its natural resources plentiful, its economy advanced and its people prosperous. The reality is different. Most of the province's three million inhabitants are very poor: they have minimal access to the formal economy, jobs are scarce, and the already large armies of unemployed, the close-packed communities that cluster in shanty towns around the urban centres, are being steadily reinforced by cross-border migrants from Mozambique and other regions that have even less to offer the work seeker.

Poverty is not, of course, exclusive to Mpumalanga, but the province has its special problems. The density of its population, and its annual rate of increase, is higher than the national average, and its productive capacity lower. Still, there are some lights on the horizon, projects and imaginative future plans designed to kick-start the regional economy, attract investment and so generate the wealth needed to provide the basic amenities of a decent life. Foremost among these prospects is perhaps the multi-billion-rand Maputo Corridor, a development pipeline that links Witbank with the Mozambique capital and coastal port by means of a new toll highway, and which will create new industries and unlock a great deal more of the mineral and agricultural riches of the region.

The coal deposits near Witbank were laid down between 200 and 250 million years ago when lush, swampy forests of primitive trees covered the sediments known to geologists as the Karoo System. As the vegetation died and decayed it formed thick banks of rotting matter on the floors of the marshes, the later layers forcing water and gas from the earlier ones, compressing them into a hard, carboniferous mass.

The Kindly Countryside

The last major South African centre on the west-east highway is Nelspruit, capital of the province, gateway to the leading tourist destinations and a handsome city of broad avenues vividly decorated by jacaranda and poinciana trees, of modern buildings, sophisticated hotels, department stores, speciality shops (the hand-woven rugs are particularly eye-catching) and suburban gardens bright with the blooms of subtropical species. Among the town's principal drawcards is the Lowveld National Botanical Garden, repository for the Witpoortjie Waterfall and a fine display of plants indigenous to this luxuriant corner of the country. Here, pathways make their leisurely way past stands of wild fig, cabbage and bizarre baobab trees, hardy aloes, ancient cycads and secluded, fern-festooned glades that shelter rare orchids. The garden, at the confluence of two rivers, is beautifully set against a backdrop of cascade and cliff.

The wider area is just as attractive. Nelspruit lies on the Crocodile River, a fairly major watercourse that rises near the mountain village of Dullstroom, on the Escarpment high above sea level, to flow 300 kilometres (190 miles) before joining the Komati River near the Mozambique border. Along its lower reaches, in the broad, fertile and pleasant valley, it nurtures plantations of pine and eucalyptus, a marvellous profusion of subtropical fruits and great groves of oranges – this is the country's second-largest citrus growing area – that, at harvest time, fill the air with their evocative scent.

A scatter of other, smaller towns share in the bounty. White River, a pleasant farming centre north of Nelspruit, is known as the 'fruit basket' of the region: it was founded shortly after the Anglo-Boer War as a settlement for ex-soldiers, and the land is still worked by smallholders to produce cut-flowers, bananas and mangoes, litchis, pawpaws, guavas, avocados, granadillas, Valencia oranges, vegetables, almonds, pecan nuts, groundnuts, and large quantities of macadamia nuts for export. In nearby Nutcracker Valley lies one of South Africa's three orange wineries, which turns out an intriguing selection of liqueurs.

Farther west, just off the main road (the N4) are the twin villages of Waterval Boven and Waterval Onder, whose names refer to their respective location 'above' and 'below' the 228-metre-high (748 feet) Elands River Falls, a splendid cascade that tumbles down the Elandsberg range – the dividing line between Highveld and the low country.

These two villages have both charm and historical significance. Waterval Boven began as the last Highveld stop on the railway line that Transvaal president Paul Kruger built, in the 1890s, at immense cost in human life – malaria, alcohol and wild animals all took their toll; one worker died, it is said, for every sleeper laid – in order to give his young Boer republic its own route to the Indian Ocean. For the railway engineers, this was the most difficult stretch of track, for here the plateau abruptly falls away, the gradients tilting to an alarming one metre in 20, which is too steep for anything but a cogged line. For the passengers, though, the views were breathtaking. The remains of the track are still visible, as is the tunnel through which it passed. Waterval Onder, a little way to the east, also has associations with Kruger: it was in this area that the ageing patriarch of Afrikanerdom briefly maintained his state residence in the last days of his presidency in 1900. In August of that year he left his beloved country for Europe, exile and death.

For generations the dreams of treasure-seekers have been animated by rumours of the 'Kruger Millions', the wagonload of bullion and gold sovereigns which the Transvaal republican government is reputed to have spirited away from the advancing British during the Anglo-Boer War. This fabulous cache (if it existed) has never seen the light of day, and some say it was hidden, by the fleeing Kruger and his faithful entourage, deep in the complex of tortuous tunnels and chambers known as the Sudwala Caves, near Nelspruit.

Overleaf: Barberton, one of the first of South Africa's gold-rush towns. In its heyday it sustained music halls, scores of bars and two stock exchanges.

TEMPERANCE HOTEL

A gathering in the main (and only) street of Pilgrim's Rest, a mining village founded when alluvial gold was discovered on Mpumalanga's high Escarpment in 1873. The first big strike, in a tiny tributary of the Motlatse River, was made by a dour Scot named Wheelbarrow Alec, one of the odder characters of the early digger community: he carried all his worldly possessions around in a barrow.

In 1974 the authorities bought Pilgrim's Rest and converted it into a 'living museum', restoring its buildings to their original (1880-1915) condition and character. Of special appeal are the old miners' cottages with their brass beds, quilted covers and pressed-steel ceilings (the cottages now accommodate visitors), the Miner's House Museum (a perfect period re-creation), the Masonic church, the bank house, the newspaper office and the Royal Hotel.

Just to the north of Waterval Boven lies the vast labyrinth of the Sudwala Caves, which has yet to be fully explored by speleologists. The cave complex was created over uncounted aeons by water eroding the surrounding dolomite layers and then continuing to seep through, the calcium carbonate in the droplets accumulating in the draught-free air to form a remarkable array of stalactites, stalagmites and speleothems.

The road south from Nelspruit leads to the now-sleepy but once vibrant town of Barberton, set in the rather lovely De Kaap Valley and named after the man who, in the 1880s, discovered one of the first reefs of gold in the area. Within weeks of the initial finds, the rudimentary diggers' camp had grown into a bustling town of some 20,000 souls, a place that boasted hotels, music halls, scores of canteens and two stock exchanges. The 'Barberton Bubble' soon burst, though, and most of the fortune-hungry citizenry drifted away to the newly opened Witwatersrand goldfields far to the west.

Mountain Paradise

Gold has also played a leading role in the history of the Escarpment. This magnificent mountain rampart, the northern extension of the awesome but no more beautiful KwaZulu-Natal Drakensberg (*see* page 124), runs from a point just beyond Nelspruit to end in the misty, forested hills of the Magoebaskloof near the Limpopo Province town of Tzaneen.

The mountains rise 1,000 metres (3,280 feet) and more above sea level, and they are spectacular in both their dimensions and their beauty. Countless millennia of wind and water erosion have carved the uplands into a dramatic jumble of buttresses, peaks and deep river valleys through which flow the Crocodile, the Olifants and their many tributaries. Biggest of the watercourses is the Olifants, which makes its way for some 800 kilometres (500 miles) from its source on the Highveld plateau near Bethal, through the Escarpment and then across the Kruger National Park to join the Limpopo in Mozambique. The hills on all sides are mantled in trees, mostly planted pines and wattles but, here and there among the ravines and on the rising ground, swathes of natural forest dense with yellowwood and ironwood, wild peach, pear and olive, cabbage, onionwood, white stinkwood, lemonwood and much else. Ferns, creepers and primeval cycads cluster closely around waterfalls exquisite in form and setting.

Much of this can be seen and savoured on the circular Panorama Route, one of several drives recommended to visitors. One variation of the route begins and ends in the pretty upland village of Graskop. It leads to some of the most attractive of the cascades; to fern- and flower-festooned picnic spots; to Bourke's Luck Potholes, a series of weirdly eroded rocks; to God's Window, the Blyde River Canyon and their sensational views; and through the canyon's nature reserve, which sustains a hugely varied plant life together with 230 or so different species of bird, including the martial and black eagle.

Other routes are as inviting. That over Robber's Pass – the name commemorates a rather comic attempt at highway robbery in 1912 – offers superb vistas. Connecting the towns of Lydenburg and Sabie is Long Tom Pass, notable for its tortuous gradients and grand views, for

Opposite page: The Lisbon Falls, one of the many lovely cascades and cataracts that grace the high Mpumalanga escarpment.

the four peaks called The Knuckles, and for The Staircase, a stretch that defeated many a wagon when transport-riders used the old trail to the east in the 1870s and 1880s.

Long Tom Pass, named after a 150-mm French-built Creusot siege gun which the retreating Boer forces used with annoying effect during the British advance in 1900. Today it serves gentler purposes, leading leisurely motorists through some of the most splendid of the country's landscapes.

Long Tom is part of the region's colonial story, which began little more than 150 years ago. Long before the white man penetrated and eventually settled the highlands, however, they were home to the Bushmen (also known as San), hunter-gatherers who used the caves and overhangs for shelter, decorating many of them with their timeless art. The Bantu-speaking people who came afterwards – precisely when the first of them began to arrive is not known, but probably early in the first millennium – were hunters too, but they also kept cattle and, in simple fashion, farmed the land. And they were also miners, excavating the red earth for iron and copper and smelting the metals for their tools, weapons and ornaments (these, indeed, are remarkably old skills in Africa: not far away, in neighbouring Swaziland, workings dating back a full 43,000 years have been found). Some years ago archaeologists unearthed the scattered shards of pottery which, when pieced together, yielded seven sinister-looking masks that evoke ancient and nameless rituals. The artefacts are now housed in the South African Museum in Cape Town, but replicas are on view locally; they can be seen in the museum at Lydenburg.

The first Europeans on the Escarpment scene were Portuguese explorers and traders, who arrived during the 16th century but made no serious attempt to consolidate their presence. They were followed, more than 200 years later, by the vanguard of the Voortrekkers, hardy and somewhat xenophobic people who resented British authority and repudiated the British way of life at the Cape, and decided to migrate across the great sunlit spaces of the interior. Their first settlement was Ohrigstad, sited in an unhealthy valley, which they quickly abandoned – though not before malaria had taken its devastating toll – in favour of a kindlier area to the south. This they named Lydenburg, which means 'town of suffering' but which, despite the grim reference, flourished to serve as the capital of their short-lived republic. The place is now a substantial and attractive centre of a prosperous forestry and mixed-farming region.

Later, in the 1870s, came the pick-and-shovel prospectors, most of them squeezed out of a Kimberley whose rich claims were being parcelled up by the big companies (*see* page 163). Denied their place on the diamond fields, they came looking for the golden lode – and found it, high up on the Escarpment, in 1873. Their first camps were Spitzkop and Mac Mac, so named for the large number of Scots among their number, and then in a secluded creek that yielded highly promising quantities of the yellow ore. This the nomadic diggers called Pilgrim's Rest for here, at last, after all the dead-end trails and faded dreams, they had found a firm base, a home.

The rush was on. Fortune-seekers came from the Escarpment camps, from Kimberley and farther afield – from Cape Town and Durban (sailors jumped ship to join the scramble) and soon enough, because news travelled fast in the world of prospectors and pan-handlers, from the Australian and Californian fields. For a time Pilgrim's Rest flourished as a lively frontier town, a self-sufficient community complete with its church, school, newspaper and hotel (the renowned Royal, whose hospitable doors are still open). But the alluvial deposits soon began to run out, the small-scale prospectors left for greener pastures and the larger enterprises moved in to mine the deeper gold. In due course these, too, became depleted and so the companies turned their attention to timber, planting the hillsides with what were to become some of the biggest man-made forests in the world. Pilgrim's Rest remains a working village (albeit a much quieter one) and forestry is still a major preoccupation, but it now derives most of its prosperity from tourism.

ABOVE: The legendary game ranger Harry Wolhuter camping out with a party of friends in the Sabi Game Reserve, later part of the Kruger National Park. Wolhuter's famed struggle with a full-grown lion – he killed it with his pocket-knife – is now part of local folklore. OVERLEAF: The Kruger's 'big five' animals. They are, in clockwise order, elephant, rhino, lion, leopard and buffalo.

The Safari Scene

The eastern faces of the Escarpment are particularly steep, plunging down 1,000 metres (3,280 feet) and more to the flattish, low-lying, searingly hot bushveld plains that occupy South Africa's north-eastern corner and extend across Mozambique to the ocean. This is big game country, a slice of relatively untouched wild Africa and location of the world-famous Kruger National Park. Founded just over a century ago by a Transvaal republican government acutely, and perhaps belatedly, aware of the devastating impact of human settlement on the natural order, the Kruger Park – and in particular its first and long-serving warden, James Stevenson-Hamilton – pioneered the conservation movement and it is now haven for more species of wildlife than any other sanctuary in Africa. The configuration of its boundaries assigns the southern part to Mpumalanga and the rest to Limpopo Province (*see* page 64), but for all practical purposes the division is a technicality since the park is run, by central government, as a single entity. It is, after all, one of the country's most valuable national assets.

The Kruger Park is the prince of South Africa's game areas, extending across almost 20,000 square kilometres (7,722 square miles, which is about the size of the American state of Massachusetts) of sun-blasted savanna and woodland countryside between the Crocodile River in the south and the Limpopo in the north.

The wild dog is a fascinating animal, though one about which much has still to be learnt, questions answered. Why, for instance, isn't the Kruger's wild dog population larger? It should be: the wildlife is well protected, prey is plentiful (more than 100,000 impala antelope, the favoured meal, roam the sunlit spaces) and the dog is a super-efficient hunter. This is one of the mysteries of the Kruger that is being probed by scientists.

Among the park's 148 species of mammal are the 'Big Five' so eagerly sought after by game-spotters, photographers and film-makers – lion and leopard, elephant, buffalo and rhino. All but the last are there in fair abundance.

Lions total some 2,500 individuals and are scattered throughout the park, though they are at their most visible on the central grasslands and around Lower Sabie in the south-east, areas where their favoured prey, the wildebeest and zebra, tend to concentrate. The leopards, though present in considerable numbers (it is estimated the park holds about 9,000 of them) are a lot less evident: they are shy animals, elusive in their solitary habits, hunters of the night who hide away in dense bush or among the granite outcrops in the hot hours of the day. Sometimes they do venture onto open ground but, with their adaptive coloration – tawny yellow dappled with black rosettes – they blend beautifully into their bushveld surrounds. Even more graceful are their cousins the cheetahs, swiftest of all land animals, able to reach speeds of up to 120 kilometres an hour (75 miles per hour) in their brief (maximum 600 metres; 1 968 feet) but dramatically explosive chases and kills. But bulk and physical strength have been sacrificed for speed, and these cats, their natural habitat reduced by human encroachment, find it difficult to compete for prey. They are among Africa's most endangered large mammal species.

Also at grave risk is the wild or Cape hunting dog, of which there are several packs in the Kruger. Long regarded by farmers and by an unaware public as pests, these splendid carnivores have been relentlessly persecuted over the decades. Despite appearances the species is not all that closely related to the domestic animal – among other differences, it has only four toes on each forefoot. Of all the predators, too, it has perhaps the most intricate social system. The hunt is a finely orchestrated collective effort, the dogs combining to run their prey to exhaustion over the grassland plains. Each member's status in the pack, its place in the hunt and its rights to the spoils, are subtly and precisely defined. The order of seniority changes over the seasons as cubs are born, adults grow old and dominance is challenged.

The rhino, too, is very much on the endangered list, already extinct in most parts of Africa and, where it survives, ruthlessly poached for its horn (much in demand in the Far East for its supposed medicinal properties). In 1970 the continent's population of the black rhino, a massive, primeval herbivore, stood at about 65,000; today fewer than about 2,400 black and 7,500 white rhino remain in the wild.

Poaching has also made savage inroads into Africa's once-great elephant herds, but their status is a lot healthier than that of the rhino. An international ban on the ivory trade, signed by 103 nations in 1989 and modified in 1997, slowed (if not halted) their decline, though the embargo had much less relevance on the southern subcontinent – in South Africa and its northern neighbours Botswana and Zimbabwe – than elsewhere. These three countries boast an excellent conservation record and their elephant populations have flourished, so much so that the herds have to be periodically culled, their superfluous animals killed off. Culling is an unpleasant, seemingly cruel process (and indeed other methods, notably birth control, are being investigated) but an ecologically necessary one since elephants can, unless their numbers are controlled, do enormous damage to the environment. A single adult bull's daily intake ranges up to

300 kilograms (660 pounds) of grass, shoots and stripped bark, and it will often topple an entire tree to get at the few tender leaves at the top. The Kruger is sanctuary to some 8,200 of these huge and (usually) gentle giants, which is about the optimum carrying capacity of the area.

The buffalo, relative of the antelope and last of the Big Five, is a large and powerful animal distinguished by the bony boss at the top of its head from which great horns curve outward and upward. It appears docile, but hunters regard it as one of Africa's most cunning and dangerous game species. Solitary males, exiled from the herd after losing a mating battle, can be especially bad-tempered and unpredictable.

These are the Kruger's bigger, more charismatic residents, and public focus on them tends to obscure the region's myriad and, in their different ways, just as fascinating forms of life. In all, the park sustains 116 kinds of reptile, 34 amphibian species, 49 fish and an impressive 505 bird species. Among the raptors are vultures, the odd-looking secretary bird, the bateleur, the imperious martial eagle and the African fish eagle, whose keening call as it hunts the rivers and dams is the quintessential sound of wild Africa. The area, too, is a treasure-house for the botanist and most especially for the lover of trees, of which there are nearly 404 different types. All these living things, together with the uncountable insects (among them 219 butterfly species) and micro-organisms, come together to create an integrated natural environment, a complex system of gene pools in an infinitely delicate balance in which the rhythms of life, fragile and wondrous, are sustained through collective dependence.

Well over a million people pass through the Kruger's eight gates each year, so the park has few pretensions to exclusivity. Some are day visitors, most stay longer, overnighting at one of the score or so rest-camps, pleasantly laid-out clusters of chalets and huts surrounded by trim lawns and handsome indigenous trees. Each of the larger places has its restaurant, shop, swimming pool, information centre, its distinctive personality. Among the more attractive are Lower Sabie, a rather old-fashioned place set among grasslands that are especially rich in game, and Satara, renowned for its birdlife. Biggest is Skukuza, 'capital' of the park and more of a village than a safari camp: it boasts a supermarket, post office, bank, doctor's surgery, auto workshop, police station, airfield and what is reputed to be the world's largest thatched building. Among the smaller venues are the private camps, available mainly to groups of people, and the bushveld camps, secluded oases designed for closer, more intimate contact with the wilderness. The camps are linked by a 2,600-kilometre (1,615-mile) network of roads, the main ones fully tarred, that lead to waterholes, viewing sites, picnic spots and to the wonders of the park's wildlife.

More exclusive, and much more luxurious, are the private reserves that sprawl across the western approaches to the Kruger Park. These areas – Timbavati, Manyeleti, Sabi Sand – are occupied by farms and game properties whose owners have clubbed together to operate commercial lodges that offer the ultimate in bushveld experiences. Here, at Londolozi (famed for its leopards) and Ngala, Motswari, Mala Mala, Mbali, Sabi Sabi, Tanda Tula and other venues, guests are treated to five-star accommodation, cuisine and service. The fences that divided the Kruger from its private neighbours, barriers originally designed to halt the spread of foot-and-mouth disease, have now been pulled down and wildlife moves freely across the boundaries.

Most of the ancient migratory paths have been closed off by human encroachment, and the animals, certainly the larger ones, are confined within relatively small conservation areas. On the drawing board, however, are advanced plans to expand their range. When these come to fruition, the Kruger will be joined with Zimbabwe's Gonarezhou conservancy, and with a large expanse of southern Mozambique, to create one huge, transnational, or 'peace' sanctuary.

James Stevenson-Hamilton

Despite the Kruger's extensive infrastructure, and the massive human presence, the park remains astonishingly unspoilt. Everything that man has done to the land, all the buildings erected, the routes laid out, takes up less than three pecent of the area. The rest belongs to nature.

BELOW: The endangered cheetah is found in the Kruger National Park.
RIGHT: A marabou stork at sunset in the Kruger Park.

Chapter Five

Free State

The Land Between Two Rivers

The Free State is a kidney-shaped region of rugged upland and grassy plain that sprawls across the high interior plateau, accommodates about 3 million people and ranks as South Africa's third largest province.

*L*ong before the coming of the early 19th-century white settlers, the high, bare, undulating countryside between the Gariep and the Vaal rivers was home to the nomadic Bushmen (also known as San), and to the Tswana and Sotho people. Later, other groups found their way into the region, driven westwards by the *Mfecane*, that devastating series of forced migrations triggered by the rise of Shaka Zulu's empire in the east (*see* page 128). Close to the Gariep River were the Griqua, a well-armed and semi-nomadic folk who had long departed the colonial Cape but who held closely to their part-Dutch heritage – to the Dutch language and the military commando system introduced by the early whites. Between the Griqua and the Sotho lived the Barolong, a Tswana group which, under its leader Moroka, received the northward-bound Voortrekkers of the mid-1830s in peace and with hospitality.

Such, in brief, is the ethnic background of what, today, is the Free State.

In the early colonial days the territory was known as Trans-Orangia, and then as the British-protected Orange River Sovereignty, and finally (in 1854), when the Boers were granted their own republic, as the Orange Free State, so named in honour of Holland's royal house. They chose Bloemfontein as their capital, though at that time it hardly deserved such titular grandness: it amounted to little more than a tiny cluster of houses whose village management board held its inaugural meeting only in 1859, and whose first 'raadsaal' (parliament) was a lowly structure that had served as the local school. The town was slow to develop.

But what gold was to do for the Transvaal, diamonds – at Kimberley, not too far away to the west – was doing for the Free State, as it is now known. Relative proximity to the Witwatersrand goldfields also contributed to Bloemfontein's prosperity, as did its strategic position astride the wagon route north from the coastal cities. By the turn of the century an English traveller was able to record that 'the town is quite one of the neatest and, in a modest way, best appointed capitals in the world. Gardens are planted with trees that are now so tall as to make the whole place seem to swim in green'.

That description remains apt enough, though today Bloemfontein is a lot larger of course. The local economy received its most powerful impetus with the post-war discovery and exploitation of the Free State goldfields, 160 kilometres (100 miles) to the north-east, and with the launch, in the 1960s, of the giant Gariep River Project. The latter brings enormous stretches of the river valley under profitable irrigation and also, through a system of canals and conduits, to the farmlands and orchards of the Eastern Cape.

Modern Bloemfontein, South Africa's judicial as well as the provincial capital, is a largish and good-looking city of some half-million souls, many of whom (around 40 percent of the working

OPPOSITE PAGE: Carpets of cosmos garland the Free State. These plants are native to Mexico, but they flourish in, and bring delicate beauty to, their adopted land. PREVIOUS PAGES: A view of Bloemfontein in its infancy, painted by the versatile artist Thomas Baines (1820-75). PREVIOUS PAGES INSET: The rugged landscape around Clarens, in the eastern Free State.

ABOVE AND OPPOSITE: The concentration camps, part of Kitchener's scorched-earth campaign, were intended to deny sustenance to the elusive Boer guerillas. Crowded and unhygienic conditions took a devastating toll on the Boer women, children and old people interned in the camps.

population) are employed in social, community and government services. It also supports hundreds of light industries and the largest railway workshops in the country. Within its precincts are the fourth of the republican raadsaals, a fine piece of architecture, completed in 1893, that reflects the Classical revival (it is Greek in detail, Renaissance in form); the modern and rather splendid Sand du Plessis theatre complex, and the University of the Free State, which, although a child of the English-speaking Grey College and the University of Cape Town, has functioned as a largely Afrikaans-medium institution.

On Monument Road stands an imposing obelisk and the statues of two women, one holding a dying child, the other gazing across the Free State plains. This is the National Women's Memorial, erected in honour of those who died in the concentration camps during Britain's bitter confrontation with the Boers a century ago. These places of horror were part of British commander-in-chief Lord Kitchener's wider strategy to starve the elusive Boer guerilla commandos into submission, a policy that involved the wholesale destruction of farmlands and homesteads

Altogether, 27,000 whites and an uncounted number of blacks perished within the fenced enclosures of the concentration camps established by the British during the Anglo-Boer War, prompting leading Westminster politician David Lloyd George to predict that 'a barrier of dead children's bodies will rise up between the British and Boer races in South Africa'.

and the incarceration of thousands of rural families. The concentration camps were designed not to exterminate but to intern (even, in some respects, to protect), but lack of proper organization, poor food and overcrowding in unhygienic conditions triggered vicious epidemics of measles, enteritis and amoebic dysentery which, in the latter part of 1901, pushed the death rate up to an appalling 34 percent.

At the base of the obelisk lie the remains of Emily Hobhouse, perhaps the most persistent of the British voices – and there were many – to be raised against both the war and its devastating effect on the multitudes made homeless by Kitchener's scorched-earth campaign. She visited South Africa to inspect the white camps (of the black ones she remained either ignorant or uncaring) and returned to England to publicize, very effectively, what the Liberal political opposition came to call 'methods of barbarism'. Nevertheless, until her reports were validated, she was widely reviled by her own people. Kitchener called her 'that bloody woman', denied her access to the camps on her second visit, and then deported her under martial law.

The charming upland village of Clarens is girded around by the splendour of the mountains, its Lombardy poplars shading some lovely homes. Photographers beat a path to this exquisite place; so too do artists and other creative folk in search of peace and beauty.

None of this deterred Emily: she returned after the war, organized relief funds, launched a home-industries scheme, and wrote powerfully of the sufferings of the Boer people. Late in her life, poverty-stricken and ailing, she bought a small house in Cornwall with donated funds, most of them collected in the then Orange Free State, and on her death her ashes were brought to South Africa to be interred at the Memorial.

The Golden Highlands

The Free State is a land of striking physical contrasts. The vast prairielands of the south and west tend to be dry, scenically monotonous, devoid of trees and indeed of any very distinctive natural features, though the landscape is punctuated here and there by dolerite ridges and rocky outcrops. A bleak country, the great lonely spaces swept by bitter winds in winter, dust-blown and baked to brown hardness in summer, yet imparting a special kind of beauty. But, for all that, it is blessed with great riches: the soils are deep and good and the sweet, nourishing grasses sustain herds of fat cattle and more than half South Africa's 28 million head of sheep. Towards the north, in the lands drained by the Vaal River, the broad acres are given over to maize and wheat.

Quite different is the terrain of the province's eastern parts: here the land rises in a spectacular series of sculpted, Arizona-type rock formations, many of them steep-sided and flat-topped, all of them vividly coloured. This, too, is a highly productive region, kind to the growers of maize, wheat, soya, sorghum and sunflowers. The higher-lying areas are responsible for about 40 percent of the national potato crop – and 90 percent of the country's cherry harvest, most of which is grown and gathered around Ficksburg. The farmlands around the town, set against the majestic heights of the Malutis, also yield plums, peaches and apricots. But it is the cherry that delights the eye: in springtime Ficksburg's streets and the countryside around are washed by frothy oceans of their delicate blossoms.

To the north-east lies the Golden Gate Highlands National Park, which gets its name from the massive, remarkably hued yellow-gold sandstone hills that line the valley of the Little Caledon River. This was South Africa's first scenic national park (it was proclaimed in 1963) and fully deserved its pioneer status: the dramatic, often weirdly weathered buttresses, peaks and ridges come in a multitude of subtle shades, sandstone and iron oxide combining to create a wonderland of reds, oranges, yellows and golden browns. Especially eye-catching are Mushroom Rocks – formed by erosion of the lower sandstone material, leaving the surrounding, harder quartzite cap intact – and Cathedral Cave, a 60-metre-deep (200 feet) chamber carved from the rock by a once-powerful river that still flows in the rainy season. When it does so, it plunges through a hole in the ceiling to create a strikingly unusual waterfall.

Most visitors to the park come mainly for its extraordinary landscapes, but it also has an impressive wildlife complement: mountain reedbuck and oribi have long been in residence and other species, among them eland, red hartebeest, zebra, black wildebeest and springbok, have been reintroduced. Avian life includes raptors such as the bearded vulture, or lammergeyer, the blue crane (South Africa's national bird), the jackal buzzard and the black eagle. The park's

Opposite page: Rain-clouds gather over the high plains of the eastern Free State. Windmills tap the good water that lies beneath the ground.

Sir Harry Smith

plants add to the interest: the stark terrain is softened by a veld sometimes bright with fire-lily, watsonia, red-hot poker and arum lily, and by the willows and poplars that decorate the river banks. Both these trees are exotics, but are allowed to flourish – contrary to strict conservation practice – because they have been there for a long time, and because they are a joy to behold.

Harrismith, at the eastern extremity of the province, stands astride the main highway connecting Johannesburg and Durban, a route busy with coast-bound traffic in the high-summer holiday season. The town was named in honour of Sir Harry Smith, veteran of Wellington's Peninsula campaign and of Waterloo and, later, flamboyant governor of the Cape Colony, who created the British-controlled Orange River Sovereignty and, when the bitterly resentful Boers took up arms, personally led his troops to victory at the battle of Boomplaats. His Spanish wife Juanita is commemorated in the names of two other South Africa towns: Ladismith in the Western Cape, and Ladysmith, across the provincial border in KwaZulu-Natal and scene of the Anglo-Boer War's grimmest siege (*see* page 119). Nature lovers passing through Harrismith should, if they can spare the time, break their journey here for a few exploratory hours: in the local wild-flower reserve more than 1 000 plant species found on the high Drakensberg range are on display; and the scenically outstanding QwaQwa Park (which will soon join with the Gold Gate Highlands park to create a magnificently scenic super-sanctuary) lies not too far away.

Under the apartheid regime QwaQwa was a 'semi-independent' territory, the smallest and poorest of the 'national states' dreamt up by the social engineers of Pretoria and designated the homeland of the South Sotho folk or, rather, two specific sections of the group, the Kwena and Tlokwa. In rough translation the name, rather ironically, means 'whiter than white', which refers not to its inhabitants but to the pale sandstone hills of the region. This poverty-stricken area, though, offers riches that have nothing to do with material things – a wealth of tradition, which resides in the lore and lifestyle, customs and convictions of the people, and is most visible in the brightly decorated homes that dot the grasslands and in the carpets, wall-hangings, pottery and basketware crafted by their occupants. There is also a wealth of natural beauty in the surrounding mountains, their yellowwood and tree-fern forests, deep ravines and undulating plains.

Welkom, north of Bloemfontein and not far from the Vaal River, is the centre of the Free State goldfields, which produce about a third of the country's output of the yellow metal though its mines have been struggling of late. The town, founded in the later 1940s, is neatly laid out, well endowed with malls, public gardens and wildlife sanctuaries. The latter focus on lakelets and dams fed by water from the underground mine-workings, and support an extraordinarily prolific bird life that includes a multitude of pink flamingoes together with Egyptian geese, Muscovy ducks (maccoa), sacred ibises and marsh owls.

The Vaal rises on the western slopes of the Drakensberg and flows south-westwards to demarcate the Free State's borders with the provinces of Mpumalanga, Gauteng and North-West before joining the Gariep River in the Northern Cape. It has a total run-off of 5.6 billion cubic metres (198 billion cubic feet), and is profitably harnessed for irrigation, for hydroelectric generation, and for recreation. The Vaal Dam offers a vast stretch of deep, limpid, bilharzia-free water to anglers, water-skiers and powerboat enthusiasts.

Previous pages: A golden field of sunflowers, grown for the oil in their seeds, ripens in the hot summer sun.

Among the larger centres along the river's banks are Parys, situated on a part of the main watercourse which has divided into an intricate network of streams and rivulets that flow around well-treed islands; and Sasolburg, site of the country's first synthetic fuel plant. This enterprise was launched in 1950, using techniques developed in the 1930s by the brilliant industrial scientist Hendrik van Eck, and it remains a leader in the field, representing the world's only commercially viable oil-from-coal venture. Much of its success, though, has been achieved with the government's – that is, the taxpayer's – help. By-products of the process are used in the manufacture of fertilizers, plastics and synthetic rubber. But for all that, the town of Sasolburg is blessed with open spaces and more than 70,000 trees, including 14 different kinds of oak.

The province's southern border is the Gariep River and its most notable dam is the Gariep (formerly the Hendrik Verwoerd). This is the country's largest reservoir, covering 374 square kilometres (144 square miles) of grassland countryside. On the northern shore lies the Gariep Nature Reserve, haven for South Africa's largest herd of springbok, together with black wildebeest, mountain reedbuck, Cape mountain zebra and other large herbivores. Oviston Nature Reserve, on the southern side, nurtures game for translocation to havens elsewhere; the animals of the Tussen-die-Riviere game farm to the east, at the junction of the Gariep and Caledon rivers, are the product of an unusually impressive re-stocking exercise launched in the 1970s.

Before the arrival of the white farmers and hunters with their passion for killing, the vast, bare plains of the region supported many millions of game animals. They have now all but disappeared from the open country, but the Gariep Dam is flanked by a number of conservation areas in which the wildlife, most of it reintroduced, is well protected.

A horse-drawn cart crossing the veld is part of the enduring rhythm of rural life in the Free State.

Chapter Six

KwaZulu-Natal

Beneath the Dragon's Mountain

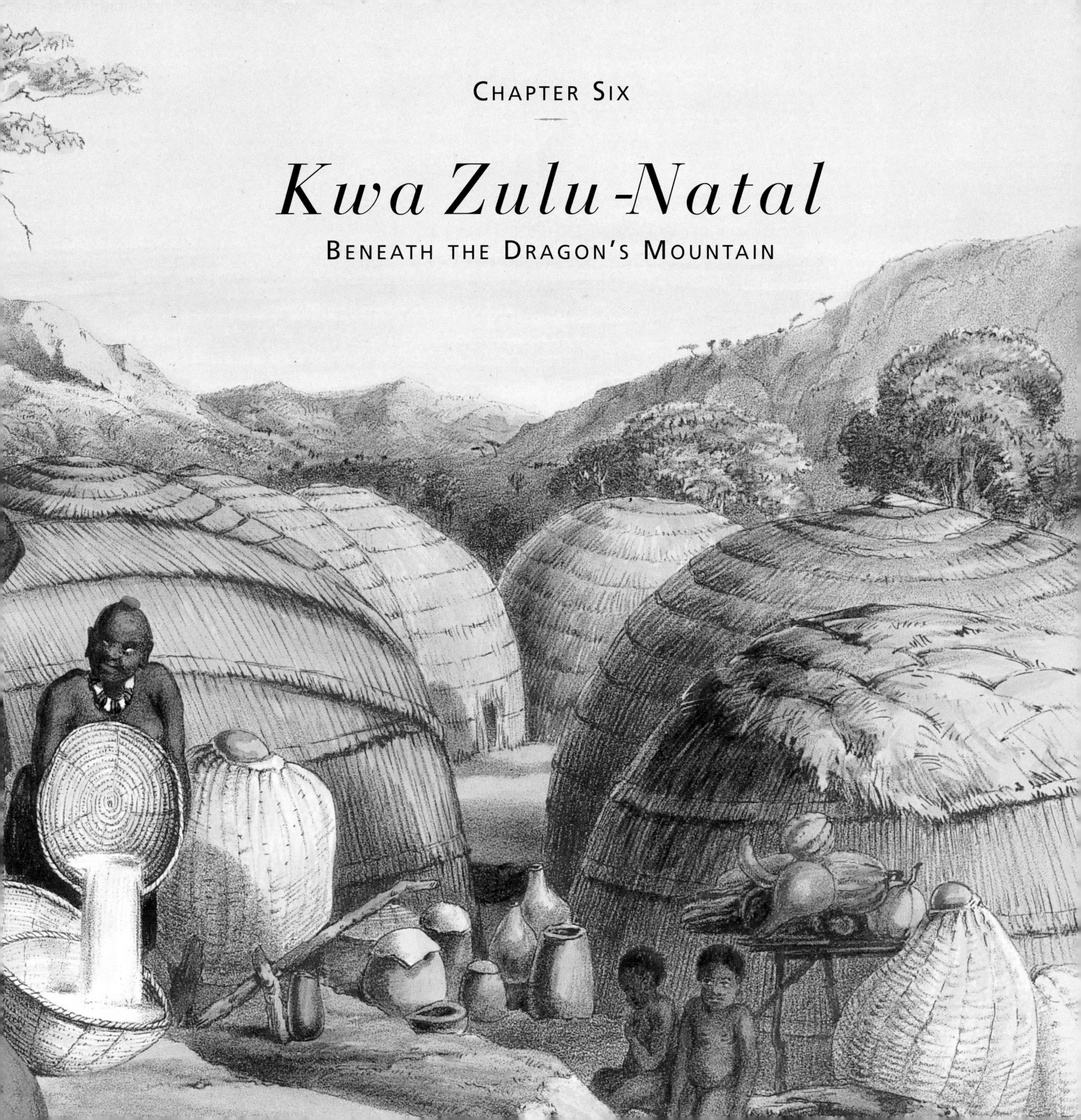

Durban, third largest of South Africa's conurbations, is one of the great port cities of the southern hemisphere. It is also regarded as the country's premier playground, a claim under serious challenge from Cape Town. Still, Durban is holding its own in the tourism stakes and will probably continue to do so, simply because it has so much to offer.

*D*urban lies in a subtropical region, humid, warm for most of the year, torrid for some of it, enveloping the leisure-bent visitor in a cocoon of heat and sun-kissed hedonism. The pleasures and attractions it offers are enjoyed in surroundings that are almost theatrical in their luminosity. It is a large city, blessed with a balmy climate, lush plantings, broad sands, and the great rollers of the blue Indian Ocean, and it is well equipped to receive and spoil the holidaymaker.

Durban's surf and its beaches, packed with sun-worshippers, are world famous. Behind the beachfront is the Golden Mile, a six-kilometre (four-mile) strip of shoreline dedicated wholeheartedly to pleasure. The Mile is well named. It really does glitter – with nightspots, entertainment centres, hotels, amusement parks, piers, pools, pavilions, markets and malls and a myriad eateries. For all that, though, its creators have kept good taste firmly in mind, building into the overall design trim lawns, graceful fountains, paved walkways and much else of beauty.

Small Beginnings

Durban, named in honour of Cape colonial governor Sir Benjamin D'Urban (1834-37), grew up around what is arguably the southern hemisphere's finest natural harbour. The first European to see the spacious, almost entirely enclosed bay was the Portuguese maritime explorer Vasco da Gama, who assumed it to be an estuarine lagoon at the mouth of a large river and, because he had sailed along the coastline at Christmastime (the year was 1497), named it Rio de Natal.

It was three centuries after Vasco da Gama discovered Durban before white men made the first serious attempt to colonize what, by then, had become part of Shaka's new and explosively expanding Zulu empire. In 1824 two small groups of adventurous souls, led by British naval officer Francis Farewell and his deputy Henry Fynn, stepped ashore intent on conducting a profitable trade in animal hides and elephant ivory. They managed to extract a generous (though rather vague) land concession from the Zulu king, and built their rudimentary settlement among the mangroves and marshlands of the bay's steamy shoreline.

Durban was slow to develop: a decade after this first landing its permanent residents were still just thirty strong. Nor were the following years much livelier. But in 1845 the territory was annexed to the Cape Colony and a steady stream of immigrants, some of them gentleman farmers and aristocratic second sons, most of them solid, lower middle-class Britons, began to arrive on the golden shores of the Empire's newest possession. By 1854, when the town's white population stood at 1,600, the Rev William Holden, a second-time visitor to Durban, was

OPPOSITE PAGE: The soaring heights of the Drakensberg. This mountain rampart, the most striking segment of South Africa's Escarpment, guards KwaZulu-Natal's north-western boundary. PREVIOUS PAGES: Zulu women making beer, from an 1849 painting by George Angas. PREVIOUS PAGES INSET: A white rhino and her calf in the Hluhluwe-Imfolozi Park.

Indian contract workers, or 'indentured labourers', landing at Durban's docks on their way to the sugar plantations. Most of them chose to make Natal their permanent home.

astonished at the change. 'Instead of a solitary house here and there, hid in thick bush', he wrote, 'there are now many buildings erected, both substantial and handsome.' A railway, South Africa's first, made its appearance in 1860, and by the end of the century, after decades of costly dredging to remove the Bay's notorious sandbar, the harbour had been opened to ocean steamers.

With these improvements came rapid expansion of the economic base, and today Durban's bay is the setting for Africa's premier trade outlet. The harbour, ninth largest in the world, is still almost completely landlocked, its southern waters bounded by an 8-kilometre-long (5 miles) wooded headland called The Bluff and its northern ones by a narrower, lower-lying spit known as The Point, but the big ships have trouble-free access to a vast complex of quays, cranes, trains and storage facilities that process close on 50 million tons of cargo each year. Sugar and subtropical fruits, maize, manganese, coal and anthracite are major export commodities.

The Berea was so called by an early missionary who, after being rejected by the Zulus, made his way to the infant settlement and built a mission station on the slopes; the name is a reference to St Paul, who came to Berea, in Macedonia, where the people 'received the Word with all readiness of mind'.

Faces of Durban

The city proper, 300 square kilometres (116 square miles) in area, extends along the south coast, northwards to the Mgeni River and inland, over a ridge known as the Berea. At the top of the ridge is the Durban campus of the University of Natal; beyond, to the west, are suburbs that rise to a plateau high enough to enable occupants of its fashionable residential areas to escape the worst of the summer heat and humidity.

Greater Durban is reputed to be the world's fastest growing conurbation, its numbers expanding more quickly than those of Calcutta, Cairo, Mexico City or São Paolo. But expanding for much the same reasons. By far the greater majority of its citizens are Africans of Zulu stock, migrants from a countryside that has been troubled by political violence, and which is becoming less and less capable of meeting their minimum economic needs. The armies of the poor have been congregating in their thousands in ramshackle settlements on the western city fringes, and their integration into the urban mainstream is the principal challenge facing Durban's metropolitan authorities.

The Durban area is also home to large numbers of Indian people, many descended from the indentured labourers brought in during and after the 1860s to work on the great sugar cane plantations of the coastal belt. Each was initially bound by a three-year contract, followed by another five years as a 'free' worker, after which he could choose between repatriation to his homeland or permanent residence and a small patch of Crown land. The majority opted for the latter, and over the following decades they were joined by thousands of their compatriots, ordinary immigrants (known as 'passenger Indians') who were British subjects and could travel more or less freely within the Empire.

The local Indian communities have remained remarkably integrated, holding fast to their cultural heritage, their religions, languages, music, cuisine and (though to a declining extent) their modes of dress. Most came from the Madras area, but there were also traders from the state of Gujarat, and it was to look after the interests of these people – successful folk whose very flair for business had caused resentment among Durban's white establishment – that a young lawyer named Mohandas Gandhi came to Durban.

Gandhi arrived in 1893, a time when the colonial government was busy introducing laws that threatened Natal's Indian society. Among the measures were the Indian Immigration Bill, designed to repatriate indentured labourers; the Franchise Amendment Bill, limiting the vote to those who already had it, and the Dealers' Licences Bill, which effectively denied Indian merchants the right to trade. All this and much else in the way of legalized persecution persuaded Gandhi, better known today as the Mahatma ('Great Soul'), to remain and lead the political struggle. He became a key figure in the founding of the Natal Indian Congress in 1894 and thereafter campaigned vigorously, largely through letters and petitions. His work was briefly interrupted by the outbreak of the Anglo-Boer War (1899-1902), during which he led a team of battlefield stretcher-bearers (they were wryly known as 'body snatchers'), but was soon enough back in political harness.

The Immigration Act of 1913 provided the final and most powerful impetus for the passive resistance movement in South Africa. Up to this time Gandhi's protest policy had been moderate, even elitist (it had been conducted largely on behalf of the merchant class), but he now sought and gained support among ordinary Indian labourers, organizing massive strikes on the coalfields of northern Natal. The stoppages spread to the sugar cane plantations and other sectors; there were riots and widespread incidents of arson. On three occasions Gandhi was arrested, on the last drawing a nine-month prison sentence.

MOHANDAS GANDHI

Gandhi's newspaper, Indian Opinion, *which was printed at and distributed from his Phoenix self-help settlement near Durban, added to his armoury, spreading his evolving philosophy of 'passive resistance', more correctly known as* satyagraha *(loosely translated as 'keeping firmly to the truth'). In essence, this held that nothing can be attained through violence, and that love and truth will eventually prevail.*

Decades ago, the writer and traveller H.V. Morton said there was 'an air of musical comedy, or of a film set about Durban. The light is just a little too strong and white to be sunlight, the flowers are a little too bright to be real, the flamboyant trees seem too exotic to be genuine ...'. He wrote that in 1948, when Durban was still growing and had yet to don its full finery.

The unrest, however, prompted General Jan Smuts, South Africa's interior minister at the time, to appoint a commission of enquiry, and in June 1914 the two men reached an agreement that produced the Indian Relief Act. Gandhi, believing his work complete and well aware that the Empire might soon be at war with Germany, returned to his native land and eventually, after a three-decade struggle against British rule, led India to its independence. Before Gandhi departed for India, he told Smuts that 'complete satisfaction cannot be expected until full civic rights have been conceded the resident population', but there was mutual respect and, oddly enough, even personal affection between the two political antagonists – the conservative Afrikaner soldier and the ascetic Indian pacifist. While in prison, Gandhi had made Smuts a pair of leather sandals, a gift the latter treasured all his life long.

Today about half the country's Indian population of about a million live in the wider Durban area, their presence a strikingly attractive feature of the city scene. Walk a few blocks west of the central area and you will find yourself in an exotic, colourful and wholly unexpected environment. Here the air is aromatic, sharpened by the pungent scents of sandalwood, incense, spice and rose, filled with the semi-tonal sounds of the tanpura, the beat of Eastern drums and the languages of Bombay and Madras. The streets and alleyways are animated, bright with saris, noisy with the raucous voices of traders, their shops crammed to their low ceilings with silks and satins, silverware, brass, ceramics, gold and a huge inventory of more prosaic goods. Especially inviting is the Victoria Street Market, which beckons the shopper and browser with its cornucopia of Eastern foods and its fresh fish and produce stalls, its fabrics, jewellery and craftware.

There is, of course, more than this to Durban's Indian heritage. Much of it is devotional and hidden from outsiders. Some, though, is readily accessible. On Grey Street stands the largest mosque in the southern hemisphere, its domes afire with reflected light at sunrise and sunset. Farther out, in the suburbs, are other focal points of Indian culture. Foremost among Hindu religious centres is probably the Hare Krishna Temple of Understanding, designed and built by the International Society of Krishna Consciousness. The structure, in Chatsworth some way south of the city, is an eye-catching mix of Eastern and Western architecture, featuring ornate and soaring towers, a moat, landscaped grounds and, inside, beyond the pink-and-white marbled foyer, an enormous, hexagonal, bare and beautiful temple chamber. To the north of Durban lies the Phoenix settlement, a quiet and contemplative place holding relics and reminders of Gandhi.

The Enchanting Midlands

Durban is by far KwaZulu-Natal's largest urban area, but it is not the provincial capital. That status has for decades belonged to Pietermaritzburg, set in the misty uplands some 90 kilometres (55 miles) inland. In the 1990s, however, there was some doubt about where precisely the seat of provincial government should be sited: Ulundi, historic centre of Zulu authority, made a strong bid for a change of venue but eventually lost out.

Lovely trees of many kinds mantle the hills and valleys of Pietermaritzburg's suburbs; parks and gardens blaze with the brightness of azalea, rose-bush and camellia. Red-brick Victorian buildings – the most prominent among them the City Hall, completed in 1893 on the site of the old Voortrekker parliament – are a pronounced feature of the central area, as are the wrought-iron railings, the antique stores and the bookshops.

Pietermaritzburg is an attractive, rather old-fashioned city that, as one writer put it, 'wears its air of grace and quality with becoming ease'.

The town was founded in 1838 by the Voortrekkers, who saw Natal's green and pleasant countryside as their promised land. They named the settlement for two of their leaders, Piet Retief, done to death (together with his 100-strong advance party) by Zulu king Dingane on the slopes of KwaMatiwane, the bloody 'hill of execution', and Gert Maritz, who died of fever in the same year. Before the battle of Blood River – an unequal contest in which the flower of Zulu manhood wilted before the guns and laagered discipline of the Trekkers – the Boers had vowed that should the Almighty grant them victory they would erect a church as a memorial in His honour. This duly made its appearance, a small, white, gabled building that now functions as one of the city's museums. But the Voortrekker republic of Natalia lasted just half a decade before the British took control of territory and town and, for the most part, Pietermaritzburg's character has been shaped not by its Dutch-speaking origins but by its British colonial past.

Perhaps the most striking physical feature of the wider area is the Valley of a Thousand Hills, a majestic series of gorges and high slopes that follows the course of the Mgeni River for some 65 kilometres (40 miles), from the distinctively flat-topped sandstone Natal Table Mountain to the east of Pietermaritzburg, down to the ocean just to the north of central Durban. The valley is heavily populated in parts, magnificently wild in others, and everywhere a luxuriant green, counterpointed by the stridency of arum and fire lilies, red-hot pokers, scarlet aloes and Mexican sunflowers. A scenic road leads along the southern rim.

The country to the north is known as the KwaZulu-Natal Midlands, an enchanting, often mist-wreathed region of rolling hills and emerald valleys that lies between the high and craggy Drakensberg on one side and the humid coastal belt on the other. The visual beauty, the apparent tranquillity, is deceptive, however, for during much of the 19th century the region served as a battleground, a vast cockpit in which Zulu, Boer and Briton fought bitterly for mastery of the land. The most destructive of the conflicts was the last. Here, on and around the banks of the Thukela River and farther north, were waged some of the bloodiest battles of the Anglo-Boer War as the closely packed, parade-ground British regiments tried to break the river-line, and were cut to pieces by the Mausers of Louis Botha's well-entrenched riflemen. Today, military enthusiasts come from afar to tour the old fields – Elandslaagte, Colenso, Talana Hill, Spioenkop. And other killing grounds, among them Blood River and Isandlwana, Rorke's Drift and Ulundi.

Many Midlands towns also feature in the annals of warfare, most notably Weenen, Estcourt, Colenso, Dundee and Ladymith, which suffered the harshest of the Boer sieges. Ladysmith was described by a survivor in 1900 as 'an awful hole, celebrated for heat, dust, storms, wind and insects'; dysentery and typhoid fever took a devastating toll of its British garrison and civilian residents; at one point the hospital, built to house 300, was crammed with 2,000 patients. Today these towns are pleasant places, girded in greenery and as peaceful as can be in a province that has been riven by party-political strife. Largest of them is Newcastle, close to the north-western border and a substantial industrial centre that revolves around coalfields and steelworks.

Pietermaritzburg in the 1920s. The city, an hour's drive inland from Durban, was born of the Afrikaner passion for freedom from colonial control but grew up in a very English way, and little remains of its Boer origins. British immigrants and their progeny wove the social fabric; pro-British sentiment provided the political dynamic, and it was not so long ago that the Union Jack was still being hoisted each morning outside the most prestigious of the local clubs.

Queen Victoria still gazes imperiously over what was once the most loyal of her domains. Pietermaritzburg served as the capital of Natal Colony, and the ruling establishment (its assembly building can be seen in the background) fought long and hard to retain the region's colonial status in the years before Union in 1910. And the mood persisted: popular opposition to the new South African flag in the 1920s was always vocal, and occasionally violent.

The High Drakensberg

Mont-aux-Sources is a hugely imposing feature that rises 3,048 metres (10,000 feet) above sea level at the northern end of the main Drakensberg sequence. On one side it overlooks the sandstone hills of the Free State, and on the other the plains of KwaZulu-Natal. The name, which means 'mountain of springs', was conferred by two adventurous French missionaries, the reverends Daumas and Arbousset, as early as 1836, which is about the time the Voortrekker vanguard set out in search of their eastern homeland. The Frenchmen had made their approach from the west, negotiating the formidable heights of Lesotho's 'roof of Africa' to reach the precipitous cliffs of the KwaZulu-Natal Drakensberg, and here they observed that an unusual number of rivers and streams – the 'springs' – rose on the massif. Included among the headwaters are those of the Elands and Tugela. The eastern face of Mont-aux-Sources is curved, and when viewed from below, resembles an amphitheatre – which in fact is what it is called. Over its rim the Tugela River plunges in a series of dramatic cascades, one of which is a sheer, 183-metre (600-feet) drop, and in deep winter the uppermost section freezes into a spectacular, stalactite-like sheet of ice.

ABOVE: The Drakensberg foothills enchant the eye, beckon the hiker and the lover of flowers. The region sustains nearly a thousand different kinds of plant. OPPOSITE PAGE: The Thukela River winds its way down from the high Amphitheatre on the first stage of its journey to the Indian Ocean. PREVIOUS PAGES: Himeville's Kenmo Lake in its autumn glory (left); two views of the misty enchantment of the Mooi River area (right).

The Drakensberg range, known to the Zulu as uKhahlamba, is the grandest segment of South Africa's Great Escarpment, the high ridge that, rather like a gigantic horseshoe, runs around the country's perimeter to divide the narrow coastal belt from the interior plateau. KwaZulu-Natal's 'Berg area is protected within the uKhahlamba-Drakensberg Park, a World Heritage Site.

For those who have not been to the Drakensberg, the region evokes intimidating images of balaclavas, sheepskin jackets and snowbound isolation. And indeed the weather around the rugged crests and higher slopes can be violent and treacherous: storms of heroic proportions will suddenly erupt, shrouding the heights in thick, swirling raincloud. In the cold months they lie deep in snow. But only the climbers and the more intrepid hikers experience these conditions; ordinary visitors confine themselves to the countryside below, the gentler foothills where the climate is equable for most of the time, and where there are resort hotels that offer fine food, comfortable beds and good cheer.

Beneath Mont-aux-Sources lies the Royal Natal National Park, a broad expanse of undulating grassland, hill and cliff-face. The park is renowned for its flora rather than for its wildlife, but it does serve as haven for a variety of antelope and some magnificent birds of prey, among them the high-nesting bearded vulture and the black eagle. The Royal Natal National Park received its regal prefix after England's King George VI, his queen and the princesses Elizabeth and Margaret stopped over during their 1947 tour of the country. It also contains some impressive examples of Bushman (also known as San) rock art.

The Drakensberg was formed some 150 million years ago, which is fairly recent on the geological calendar, by volcanic convulsions that threw up unbelievably massive quantities of dark basalt lava onto what had been the sandstone plains. Thereafter, over the millennia, wind, rain and river eroded the heights, carving the 'Berg's wondrous extravaganza of buttress, ragged-edged ridge, pinnacle, saddle, balancing rock, cliff, cave and deep ravine. The formations and their peaks have evocatively descriptive names, among them the Sentinel, Champagne Castle, Devil's Tooth, the Chessmen, the Mitre, the Organ Pipes, the Bell, and for climbers they provide a superb challenge. For everyone else, they are breathtaking to behold.

Indeed there are Bushman sites scattered all over the Drakensberg uplands: among the caves and overhangs, these long-vanished folk found protection from both the often-turbulent elements and from the predations of their more aggressive fellow man. The mountains were their ideal home, close to fresh water and to the broad, game-filled grasslands to the east. Especially well endowed with Bushman art is the Ndedema Gorge, which means 'place of thunder' (an apt name since it experiences some of the Drakensberg's noisiest storms) and whose 17 'galleries' contain over 4,000 paintings, many of exceptional quality. One cave alone holds more than 1,100 individual subjects. Some fine Bushman art can also be seen in the Giant's Castle Game Reserve to the south, originally created to provide asylum for eland but now home to several other kinds of buck as well, together with a splendid array of raptors. It is also a botanist's delight: most of the Drakensberg's 800 or so species of flowering plant grow within its bounds. And, again, the scenery is memorable, with the terrain dominated by the enormous basalt wall of the Giant's Castle buttress. From here, too, you can see the looming bulk of Champagne Castle which, though at 3,375 metres (11,073 feet) is South Africa's highest peak, offers one of the region's easier climbs.

Farther to the south is the Sani Pass, the only route that breaches the Drakensberg's 250-kilometre (160 miles) length to link KwaZulu-Natal with the mountain kingdom of Lesotho. The road, which twists up in a series of dizzying switchbacks and hairpin bends, is too steep, certainly in its higher stretches, for anything but a four-wheel-drive vehicle and the donkey-carts and pack-mules of the Basotho carriers. From the summit there are panoramic views of the surrounding mountains and their wooded valleys.

Champagne Castle was given its unusual name by two rather proper British officers of Victorian times, who carried a bottle of good French bubbly with them on their way to the summit, where they intended toasting each other in celebration of their prowess but found, when they stopped to rest part-way up, that the bottle was half empty. Neither wished to accuse the other, so in true gentlemanly fashion they agreed the mountain was to blame.

Sand, Sun and Sea

Few parts of the southern hemisphere are as attractive to vacationers as KwaZulu-Natal's South Coast. The climate is almost tropical, filled with warmth and sunshine and the soothing sound of the Indian Ocean waves; the beaches are white-gold in colour, soft in texture, many fringed by iridescent estuarine lagoons, the hinterland luxuriant with green growth.

Not surprisingly, some of the country's most popular resort centres, a score and more of them, are strung out along the 170 kilometres (105 miles) of coastline between Durban and the Eastern Cape border, each with its special brand of charm.

Margate, named after and in some ways much like the English seaside town, is one of the larger and certainly the liveliest of them: it has a fine golf course, hotels, restaurants, discos, boutiques and all the other standard amenities. It is also a residential town with a solid commercial base and its own busy airport. Most of the other places are smaller, many of them even more attractive. Port Shepstone is noted for its broad estuary – of the Umzimvubu River, navigable for quite a way upstream; Uvingo for its lovely waterfall; Ramsgate for its long beach and spacious lagoon; Port Edward for the scenic beauty of the Umtamvuna Nature Reserve, its forested hills and floral species (700 of them, including 35 of orchid).

Inland from Port Shepstone is the Oribi Gorge Nature Reserve, well worth a digression to take in its spectacular, boulder-strewn canyon: carved from the sandstone layers of the Mzimkulwana River and in places nearly 400 metres deep, it carries the waters of the

LEFT: Dolphins ride the waves at Margate, liveliest of the South Coast's many resort towns.

river, and the vistas from the scenic drive along its rim are unforgettable. Wild flowers, crystal upland streams, cascades, strikingly sculpted rock formations and some lovely stands of giant stinkwoods and other indigenous trees are among the visual ingredients. The rugged terrain is home to about 270 bird and 40 mammal species, though the oribi itself, a graceful and slender-necked little antelope, is notably absent.

Similar in some respects but much quieter is the seaboard north of Durban: here, too, are enchanting stretches of sand and pretty little cliff-flanked coves and secluded clusters of holiday homes overlooking the warm, blue and generally kindly ocean. The beaches are broad and white, the shoreline graced by ilala palms, Pondoland hibiscus and by such exotics as Madagascar casuarinas and bright tumbles of bougainvillea. Biggest of the centres, and the closest one to Durban, is Umhlanga Rocks, an affluent place distinguished by its luxurious hotels, apartment complexes and a plethora of inviting restaurants. On a hill overlooking town is the headquarters of the Natal Sharks Board, a research body that studies these razor-toothed, prehistoric fish and explores ways to protect people from their predations, and vice versa. Visitors are welcome at the board's premises, where displays and audio-visual shows are laid on.

The killing field of Isandlwana where, early in 1879, a large British force was cut down almost to a man. For the Zulu, it was a great victory – but their only one of the short war.

Heritage of the Zulu

Running inland from and parallel to the main highway north from Durban is a road built along the trade route used by the early hunters and traffickers in ivory, and by the Zulu *impis* on their way south to do battle with the Pondo. Now flanked by bright-green sugar cane plantations, it leads through Tongaat – a pleasant town embowered with jacaranda and poinsettia and graceful stands of bamboo – that functions as the local sugar industry's headquarters. Dakuza (formerly Stanger), farther north, is also a sugar centre but is best known as the site on which the great Zulu king, Shaka, built his capital and where, in 1828, he was murdered by his half-brothers Dingane and Mhlangana. In the middle of the town is a small memorial garden, planted on the exact piece of ground (once occupied by a grain silo) where his body lay. This area and the lands north of the Tugela River, historically known as Zululand, are soaked in the history of this warrior people.

There was little in Zulu king Shaka's troubled childhood to portend his future as conqueror supreme and founder of a mighty African empire. His very birth (around 1788) spoke otherwise: because his mother Nandi and his father belonged to the same clan, the marriage had broken Zulu law, and Nandi was forced to flee with the six-year-old boy to the neighbouring Langeni people, with whom Shaka grew up. Mother and son, though, remained under a stigma ('Shaka' is the local word for an intestinal beetle), and in 1802, after they were expelled from the community, they found refuge with Dingiswayo's powerful Mtwetwa group. In due course the young man became, and served with outstanding ability as, one of Dingiswayo's military commanders.

In 1816 Shaka succeeded to the subordinate Zulu chieftainship – not the most promising of positions since, at that time, the Zulu were among the smallest of the 800 or so clans of the eastern Nguni (it numbered a bare 1,500 members). But his genius, and the ruthless discipline he imposed, quickly transformed both the structure and the power of his small band of followers.

Shaka's first priority was the reorganization of his tiny army, its weapons and fighting methods. And Shaka fought not just to win, but to exterminate – a new approach to warfare on the veld.

In 1817 Dingiswayo died and the road was open for expansion. Shaka swiftly overcame the smaller neighbouring clans, including the Langeni who, during his childhood, had heaped such humiliation on him and his mother (his special Langeni enemies were impaled on the fences of their kraals), and his *impis* went on to rout the powerful Ndwandwe and Qwabe people before turning on the confederation of Nguni clans to the south. The conquered lands were devastated, the villages burnt, the survivors either absorbed into the Zulu nation or put to flight.

Shaka's military exploits were largely confined to the region between the Drakensberg and the sea, but they had a ripple-like effect which spread with hugely disruptive force throughout the subcontinent in a sequence of massive migrations known as the Mfecane (or *Difecane*, which means 'the crushing').

Zulu ascendancy, in fact, was the principal catalyst of a series of events that were to refashion the human geography of southern Africa. The Ndwandwe split into three divisions, two of which fled northward to create their own kingdoms. Other defeated peoples fanned out across the northern interior to displace those in their way – the classic domino principle in deadly action. Still others retreated to the high mountains of modern Lesotho, where Moshoeshoe forged a new Sotho nation. Among the most notable of these 'ripples' was Mzilikazi's odyssey: ranked among Shaka's ablest commanders, he quarrelled with his sovereign and, in 1823, led his Khumalo warriors away from Zululand, first to what is now the Mpumalanga region and then westward, conquering and absorbing the local Sotho communities until he had created a 20,000-strong 'raiding kingdom'. He was eventually defeated by the Voortrekker vanguard, the Boers who were infiltrating the northern areas, and crossed the Limpopo River to establish the militaristic Ndebele state in the south of today's Zimbabwe.

A dramatic new chapter in Shaka's story, the final one, opened in 1827 when his mother Nandi died. Grief-stricken to the point of mental derangement, he set out on an orgy of destruction. All pregnant women, together with their husbands, were put to death; all milch cows (milk was basic to Zulu diet) were slaughtered so that, as Donald Morris writes in *The Washing of the Spears*, 'even the calves might know what it was like to lose a mother'. Then, in the following year, Shaka sent his warriors on a raiding foray to the south and, on their return, immediately ordered them to the far north. This proved too much for his exhausted and fearful subordinates, and in September of 1828 he was assassinated by his two half-brothers.

The Zulu state remained awesomely powerful, but its pre-eminence was to prove short-lived. The first white colonists had gained a foothold in 1824 (*see* page 113) and, although they were small in number and peaceable by inclination, other and more aggressive whites were soon to follow. Dingane, who succeeded Shaka, fought a bloody, courageous but in the end unsuccessful war against the Voortrekkers; his successor Mpande then overthrew him (with Trekker help) to rule the region over a three-decade period during which the Zulu, now confined to their lands to the north of the Tugela, lost much of their power and more of their territory to the encroaching settlers.

THE PRINCE IMPERIAL

Among the more celebrated casualties of the Anglo-Zulu war was Eugéne, Prince Imperial of France and only son of Emperor Napoleon III and his wife, Empress Eugénie. The young officer, a member of British commander Lord Chelmsford's staff, was ambushed and killed by a Zulu patrol near Ulundi on 1 June 1879. The body was taken to England for burial; a grief-stricken Eugénie later visited the site of her son's death.

Shaka, the great Zulu king, introduced the long-bladed, short-handled stabbing assegai, which forced warriors into close combat (until then, 'battles' often amounted to little more than a token exchange of throwing spears, the weaker side retiring after the formalities were complete). He refined the age-graded regimental system, the Amabutho, which other Nguni groups to the north had successfully created and used, so that his soldiers now lived with men of their own standing, in their own quarters, with their distinctive markings and regalia. Above all, he developed Zulu battle tactics to a fine science. The regiments in the field, collectively known as the impi, were divided into four groups, arranged roughly in the shape of an ox: the strongest of the units, the 'chest', clashed head-on with the enemy; the second and third, the 'horns', flanked and encircled them; the fourth remained in reserve.

Zulu male ceremonial regalia, which in some places and at some times is still worn, is both colourful and impressive, comprising patterned rawhide shield, either spear or fighting stick, a kilt of animal-hide 'tails', fur and feathers, ostrich-plumed headdress or, if the man is married, a simple head-ring. The ears are covered with small, decorated panels, the lobes pierced to 'open up the mind'. Both the women and the men adorn themselves with beadwork – a great deal of it on gala occasions – around hips, arms, neck and ankles. The stitched-together designs are symbolic as well as intricate, each pattern and colour holding a subtle message. Colours have precise meanings, though these differ from area to area; they tell of joy, sadness (usually red, for the weeping of eyes), of love (white) and esteem (blue). Black signifies marriage.

Traditionally, Zulu marriages are arranged by the relatives of the bridal couple, the bride-prize, or lobola, *paid by the family of the groom. The wedding is an eleborate and joyous affair, full of colour and movement. Music is provided by the cowhide drum (sometimes supplemented by a reed pipe) and by the full-throated roar of men's voices singing in multi-part harmony, those of the women weaving their high-pitched descants over and through the pulsating beat. Massed dancers clap, sway and stamp to the songs.*

KING CETSHWAYO

The decline became a rout during the latter part of the century. In 1879 the British, intent on constructing an imperial confederation in southern Africa and conscious of the threat posed to their comfortable political schemes by an independent and still-strong Zulu monarchy, launched an invasion of the country. The ensuing war was brief: a substantial force of redcoats and local volunteers was annihilated at Isandlwana on 22 January, a battle followed almost immediately by the heroic defence of the trading store at Rorke's Drift by a handful of British soldiers (a minor but much publicized incident: eleven Victoria Crosses were awarded to restore public pride at home). Shortly thereafter a much-reinforced British army under Lord Chelmsford crushed the Zulu army at Ulundi.

The victors divided Zululand into 13 separate fragments and, in the years that followed, systematically reduced the Zulu to impotence. The region was formally annexed to Britain in 1887, and incorporated into the colony of Natal a decade later. In 1906 a section of the people rose in revolt but the insurrection, the so-called Bambata rebellion, was a mere flicker in the flame that once burned so brightly, and was swiftly extinguished.

Today the Zulu people number around seven million, many of them resident in Johannesburg and other centres of the northern industrial region. But despite urbanization and the adoption of Western ways, much of the Zulu legacy remains intact, especially in the country areas of KwaZulu-Natal. In traditional Zulu society the men assumed the duties of hunter, warrior and stockman while the women tilled the soil to produce harvests of millet (latterly maize), groundnuts, grain, sorghum and various tubers. The women also brewed the beer, fashioned baskets and pots, cleaned, gathered firewood, fetched water and generally looked after the family's daily needs. Their homes were (and still are in parts of rural Zululand) finely thatched 'beehive'-shaped huts built around a cattle compound or kraal – a sacred place into which only the daughters of the family were permitted to enter. Central to the Zulu economy were hoe-culture, hunting and, especially, cattle, though the animals were prized for their milk and hides, for the wealth they represented and for their mystical significance rather than for the sustenance they could provide. Meat was regarded as a delicacy, to be eaten only on those special occasions that merited slaughter and celebration.

Among the Zulu the religion of the forefathers coexists, quite harmoniously, with orthodox Christianity and, like the religious traditions of other African peoples, has four main ingredients. First, there is belief in a Supreme Being, who is called *Nkulunkulu*, the Great-Great-One who is the creator of all things but infinitely remote from humankind and its trivial preoccupations. Lesser deities are *Nomkhubulwana* (Daughter of Heaven), the representative of fertility and abundance, and *Inkozi Phezulu*, the paramount chief. Second, there are the more approachable ancestors, who provide the link between the dead and the living and are responsible for the day-to-day welfare of their descendants and are therefore to be respected and placated. Then there is the animistic element, which endows inanimate objects and features such as trees, rivers and boulders with spiritual content. The fourth ingredient is the spirit medium and diviner, the *sangoma*, who has direct access to the ancestors, and who will predict the future, interpret the nature of the present, and heal the body and (more usually) the mind.

On special occasions praise-singers pay homage to the chief or *induna* (or indeed to any person who merits an accolade), shouting words that are part of Zulu epic poetry, which in turn belongs to a broader, elaborate and quite magnificent body of oral literature that also embraces love-songs, legends and folklore.

In the remoter areas, visible expressions of Zulu culture are evident everywhere. However, the Ondini Historic Reserve, near Ulundi (capital of Cetshwayo's kingdom in the 1870s), provides a fascinating focus: the royal residence and kraal of thatched 'beehive' homesteads have been meticulously reconstructed; next door is the cultural museum (historical and arts-and-crafts exhibits). From here, too, visitors can set out to explore other significant sites, among them the Ulundi battle memorial; Nodwengu, King Mpande's capital from 1840 to 1872, and KwaGqohli Hill, the killing ground of Shaka's confrontation with the Ndwandwe. More commercial is Shakaland, between Eshowe and Melmoth, originally built as the set for the epic television series *Shaka Zulu* (it starred the fine local performer Henry Cele in the title role, and the British actor Edward Fox). The complex now comprises a thatched village-type hotel, where visitors can sample Zulu foods and enjoy displays by traditional dancers, potters, basket-weavers, hut-builders, herbalists and a sangoma.

Land of Lakes

Zululand's northern segment, the squarish chunk of territory lying between the Lebombo Mountains of Swaziland and the Indian Ocean, is known as Maputaland, and it is a region of striking ecological diversity. Generally low-lying, humid, lush, pristine, its 9,000 square kilometres (3,475 square miles) are a tropical wonderland of evergreen woodland, savanna, river, floodplain, lake and lagoon that sustain a remarkable variety of floral and wildlife habitats.

Maputaland's character has been determined by two major geophysical features. About 100 million years ago the area lay beneath the ocean which, over the millennia, retreated to leave a broad, sandy plain and a scatter of shallow depressions. These gathered fresh water from the rivers, among them the Phongolo and the Mkuze, to form the lakes and lakelets that are now such a spectacular feature of the region. Secondly, it is the meeting place of the tropical and subtropical zones, which accounts in part for its many distinct ecosystems and the extraordinary variety of its soils, plants, animals and birds.

Biggest of the lakes is St Lucia, centrepiece of the Greater St Lucia Wetland Park (a World Heritage Site). This is a remarkable complex, a vast (275,000-square-kilometre; 106,182-square-mile) and intricate mix of lagoon, lily-covered pan, marshland, papyrus swamp, sandy forest, palm-veld, grassland, semi-arid savanna, duneland, golden beach and reef. Lake St Lucia itself is in reality an extended estuarine system that runs parallel to the seashore, separated from it by some of the earth's highest vegetated dunes. The lake's waters are shallow, averaging just a metre in depth, and they are home to hippo and to uncountable numbers of fish, crustaceans, insects and other nutritious organisms that attract great numbers of aquatic birds – among them white pelicans, flamingoes, saddlebills, Caspian terns, spoonbills and twelve species of heron.

The St Lucia seaboard, the flanking sea and the coastline stretching up to the Mozambique border in the north, combine to form Africa's largest marine reserve. Its more prominent features are the magnificent beaches and the lovely cowrie shells they yield, the myriad tropical fish in the clear blue ocean (a paradise for scuba-divers), the offshore coral reefs (the world's southernmost) and the giant turtles that come ashore to breed.

These last are among nature's gentlest creatures, cumbersome, slow in movement, vulnerable, their only defence their hard shells, but somehow they have managed to survive virtually unchanged in form for almost 100 million years. Largest of them are the two-metre-long (6.5 feet) leatherbacks, the males of which can weigh up to 500 kilograms (1,103 pounds). The loggerhead species is somewhat smaller.

Both travel immense distances through the ocean to reach their ancestral breeding grounds, guided to their pre-ordained destination with uncanny precision by an impulse mechanism implanted at birth. Mating takes place a short distance out to sea, and then the female makes her ponderous way through the reefs and intertidal zone to the beach in quest of a scent, a distinctive smell that surrounded her when she herself was a hatchling.

Mortality among the turtles is extremely high. After a 70-day incubation period the hatchlings emerge to brave the voracious ghost-crabs of the sands and then plunge into an even more predator-infested ocean. Only one of every 500 that reach the water, it is thought, will evade death to return as an adult. And many that do survive fall victim to man's appetites and vanities: valued for their meat, their eggs, the oil in their bodies, the shells used for ornamentation and as talismans, they were slaughtered in their multitudes, and at one time both species were perilously close to regional extinction. Then, in the 1960s, the Natal Parks Board stepped in to mount a protracted, and ultimately successful, rescue operation in which shore patrols, and the active co-operation of the coastal villagers, played prominent parts. The turtles are now returning to the beaches in increasing numbers.

Maputaland's coastal region maintains two other lake systems of significance. Both lie to the north. Sibaya, southern Africa's largest and perhaps most beautiful natural expanse of fresh water, is 70 square kilometres (27 square miles) in extent and was once connected to the ocean: it still sustains ten species of now-adapted marine fish. Here, too, there are hippos and crocodiles, a scatter of elusive reedbuck in the surrounding, marshy countryside and a superb selection of birds – 280 different kinds in all, including the splendid African fish eagle. Even farther north is Kosi Bay, a chain of four lakes lying in line with the seashore. The Bay, a provincial reserve, is a tropical paradise of limpid blue water girded around by marshlands, stands of raffia, wild date and ilala palm, mangrove swamp and giant sycamore fig forest that combine to provide a haven for a fascinating variety of living forms.

OPPOSITE PAGE: An evening's quiet fishing on the still waters of Lake St Lucia, centrepiece of one of Africa's most precious wetland systems.

Both leatherback and loggerhead turtles have been nesting along Maputaland's shores for about 60 millennia, some of them beginning their long breeding journey as far afield as Kenya's Malindi area, 3,500 kilometres (2,175 miles) to the north, unerringly locating that precise stretch of sand on which they themselves were born. In the case of some individuals, this could have been 50 or more years in the past.

Maputaland's Tembe people still follow traditional ways, fishing, tilling the soil, gathering wild plants and harvesting fruit in the manner of their forefathers. The Tembe fishermen of Kosi Bay build enclosures called 'kraals', into which fish swim and are then guided through basketry tunnels into smaller enclosures, where they are speared.

OPPOSITE PAGE: The Zululand wetlands are famed for their birdlife. Seen here, in clockwise order, are the African jacana, the fish eagle and a bevy of white pelicans.

HAVENS OF THE WILD

Northern KwaZulu-Natal's humid climate, wetlands and rich flora provide ideal habitats for an enormous variety of wildlife, and its game reserves are among Africa's finest.

Until recently the sweetly grassed and well-watered area of the Hluhluwe-Imfolozi Park, once the hunting ground of the Zulu kings, was occupied by two separate reserves, both proclaimed in 1897 (which makes them southern Africa's oldest), and for their first two decades they teemed with life. But then, in the 1920s, the authorities began a large-scale, ill-conceived and near-disastrous scheme to eradicate the disease-bearing tsetse fly that was plaguing the neighbouring ranchlands, and the game was slaughtered in its thousands. In the end, though, common sense prevailed and, once chemical controls replaced the hunter's rifle, the wildlife populations stabilized. Today the Imfolozi and Hluhluwe sections sustain large and healthy complements of elephant, Cape buffalo, giraffe, zebra, blue wildebeest, lion, leopard, cheetah, wild dog, spotted hyaena, an array of antelope – and, most notably, white and black rhino.

Between them, the two sections shelter upwards of 1,200 white rhino, a remarkable figure considering that it once seemed nothing could save these massive, gentle mammals from extinction. Throughout Africa the rhino has been mercilessly hunted for their horns, highly valued in the Far East for their supposed medicinal properties, and in the Middle East for ornamentation. But the southern group, carefully nurtured by the Natal Parks Board, survived and eventually flourished to the point where, by the end of the 1960s, surplus rhino could be translocated to other reserves. Led by the celebrated conservationist Ian Player, the board's rangers and scientists pioneered the drug-darting technique to capture and move the two-ton behemoths. Small breeding herds set down in distant places have ensured the survival of the species.

Not so lucky is its cousin the black rhino, prime target of the poachers: just three decades ago Africa was home to 65,000 of the animals; today there are fewer than 3,000. But again, the remnants – those in KwaZulu-Natal and in various small reserves and game farms around the country – are assiduously protected. The 'white' rhino is actually dark grey in colour; the name is thought to derive from the Afrikaans *wyd*, or wide, a reference to the square-lipped mouth of the grazer. By contrast the 'black' rhino, a smaller and more aggressive species, is a browser, its pointed mouth well adapted to its diet of leaves and twigs.

Among the smallest and most attractive of the province's conservation areas is Ndumo in the far north, famed for the richness of its riverine life. The reserve lies on the low-altitude floodplain of the Phongolo River, and this and the flanking pans sustain a superb array of water-related birds. Altogether, some 420 different species have been recorded here, some of the tropical ones at the southern extremity of their range. The terrain is a lush, ecologically fragile compound of lakelet, marsh, reedbed, evergreen forest and fig- and fever-tree woodland. Close by, just to the east, lies the Tembe Elephant Park, which represents a belated attempt to preserve the once-numerous elephant herds of southern Mozambique. At one time they roamed freely across the border, but with the encroachment of farmlands and the sustained attrition during that country's civil war, the numbers were steadily eroded. Only some 80 of the animals survived the twin onslaught, and these and their growing progeny make up the park's population.

CHAPTER SEVEN

Eastern Cape

CRADLE OF THE XHOSA

In April 1856 a young Xhosa girl named Nongqawuse, who lived near the Kei River in the realm of paramount chief Sarhili, claimed to have seen a great vision. Speaking through her guardian and interpreter, the spirit medium Mhlakaza, she told of the will of the ancestors. The Xhosa, Nongqawuse said, were to destroy all their cattle and burn their harvests, and after such 'cleansing' the sun would become the colour of blood, a great wind would spring up, and the ancient Xhosa chiefs would rise again to drive the white man into the sea; and then the cattle-pens, the byres and the grain stores would be full again, and illness and old age would be no more.

Tragically, chief Sarhili believed Nongqawuse's prophesy, and ordered that the injunction be fulfilled. The destruction lasted 15 months and proved catastrophic, leading to mass starvation, to a precipitous decline in the Xhosa population, and to the fatal weakening of the Xhosa as a military power. Nongqawuse's prophecy, and the disaster that followed, was the culmination of a long struggle between the black and white peoples for mastery of the land in what is now known as the Eastern Cape.

Both groups were relative newcomers to the region, but the Xhosa had been the first on the scene. Some time before the 17th century a number of Nguni groups moved down from present-day Zululand to occupy the southern coastal areas, and for a hundred years or so various clans vied among themselves, without any outside interference, for territorial possession and political supremacy. But with the arrival of Dutch-speaking settlers at the Cape of Good Hope, the political map of the subcontinent was altered forever. From about the mid-1700s, the settlers encroached steadily eastwards, introducing a new and highly disruptive element into the regional equation.

Conflict was inevitable: it became endemic to the region (*see* page 20) and, in the end, just as inevitably, it was the better armed, better organized white man who prevailed. In a series of proclamations issued by the British colonial authorities between 1879 and 1894, and after a century of unrelenting confrontation punctuated by no less than nine full-scale 'frontier wars', what was left of the Xhosa lands became part of the Cape Colony.

For a brief period during the later years of the apartheid era the Xhosa people enjoyed (if that is the word) a form of limited self-government when the regime created the two 'independent republics' of Ciskei and Transkei. Although the two territories were reincorporated into the body of South Africa in the mid-1990s, they remain fairly distinct regions, largely because each has an identity rooted in its history. They had been more or less separate territorial entities since the mid-1700s, when Gcaleka, paramount chief of the amaXhosa, quarrelled with and defeated his half-brother Rharhabe, who then led his followers westwards across the Kei River into what was to become known as Ciskei (the name was coined by the 19th-century colonists, and means 'this side of the Kei').

OPPOSITE PAGE: The imposing heights of Barkly Pass in the southern portion of the Drakensberg. PREVIOUS PAGES: Thomas Baines's dramatic portrayal of the landing of the British immigrants, in 1820, on the shores of Algoa Bay. PREVIOUS PAGES INSET: A Xhosa woman in traditional dress; pipe-smoking is also part of Xhosa culture.

The Hogsback's name was apparently derived from the trio of peaks that tower over the highland plateau and which, seen from certain angles, resemble three of the bristle-backed bushpigs that snuffle around in the dense woodland depths at night.

The Traditional Lands

The Ciskei is a wedge-shaped region extending across 8,500 square kilometres (3,282 square miles) of coastal plain and hilly hinterland, home to rather more than a million people, most of whom scratch a living from the tired soil. It is a poor part of the country, overcrowded, lacking any significant mineral resources, deficient in infrastructure, still suffering from the cynicism and mismanagement of the apartheid years. There is, though, some industrial activity, centering mainly on textiles, and many of the menfolk earn a fair living in the adjacent East London and King William's Town urban areas, which lie on the territory's one-time eastern border.

And, of course, there are ambitious plans for development. Tourism features prominently in the scheme: the Ciskei region is blessed with a shoreline of exceptional beauty, a seaboard graced by lovely stretches of gently shelving beaches, by lagoons and river estuaries that teem with waders and other waterfowl, by bird-rich dune forests and unspoilt embayments that beckon the bather, scuba-diver and sporting fisherman. Inland are forested upland areas, most notably the lofty and scenically exquisite Amatola range that forms the region's coastal rampart. The thickly wooded mountains rise to an average of 1,800 metres (5,905 feet) above sea level; among their highest points is the Hogsback.

A large portion of this entrancing countryside falls within the Hogsback State Forest, a rich repository of indigenous trees, including sneezewoods and tall yellowwoods, Cape chestnuts, white stinkwoods, assegai and Camdeboo trees, knobwoods, ironwoods and wild red pears. Massive ferns grow among the tangled growth of the quiet forest floor; the booming call of the iridescent Knysna loerie, the bark of a samango monkey and the occasional furtive rustle of other elusive creatures are the only sounds that disturb the stillness. Hogsback village itself, tiny and as pretty as a postcard, amounts to just a scatter of houses, three fine country inns, an oak-lined avenue that leads to an open-air place of worship, and St Patrick's-on-the-Hill, one of Africa's smallest Christian churches.

The well-marked 104-kilometre (65 miles) Amatola Hiking Trail leads through densely wooded mountains in the far east of the province. Yellowwood, sneezewood and the ironwoods are among the many trees that grace the high slopes.

Farther east, across the narrow corridor that contains the small port city of East London, is the Transkei region, larger in extent and arguably even more attractive in its landscapes. The Transkei seaboard certainly is: the 280-kilometre-long (174 miles) Wild Coast, stretching from the Great Kei to the Mtamvuna rivers, remains a largely unspoilt wilderness famed for its sandy bays and their flanking cliffs, for the rocky reefs, the many river mouths and lagoons, and for the green hills and dense woodlands of the countryside inland. The Wild Coast is appropriately named, both for its rugged beauty and for the terrible toll its treacherous and often stormy seas have taken on man over the centuries.

On the northern shoulder of the coast lies Port Grosvenor, site of a shipwreck that still holds interest, even fascination, for the modern romantic. The 'port' – little remains of the 19th-century attempt to build a harbour – was named after the *Grosvenor*, a treasure-ship that

Cascades at Hogsback, in the Amathole range. For sheer visual delight, few places can match this little village and its surrounding mountain countryside.

came to grief in 1782. Fourteen of those on board went to a watery grave, the remaining 138, stranded without food or weaponry, embarked on the long trek west to Cape Town. Just six of them reached safety; the rest either perished or, it is thought, were taken in by and settled permanently among the black communities en route. But it was only after some 70 years had passed that the *Grosvenor*'s fabulous cargo came to light: when the bills of lading were unearthed, they showed the vessel to have been crammed with gold bullion, plates, coins, jewels and, the *pièce de résistance*, the legendary Peacock Throne of Persia. This last had been the property of Shah Jehan, a renowned Indian soldier and architect of the Taj Mahal. Then, two years after the first reports appeared, a tidy little fortune in gold and silver coinage washed ashore, and the hunt was on. A number of ambitious salvage schemes have been launched over the years since; scores of individual divers have explored the turbulent depths and some valuable and fascinating relics recovered, but the currents, the shifting sands and the razor-edged rocks are formidable obstacles, and the treasure-lode still lies hidden on the seabed, waiting to be claimed.

Among areas of special interest along the Transkei coast, and there are many, is the Hole-in-the-Wall, an enormous detached cliff that stands a little way out to sea not far from the charming village of Coffee Bay. The hole itself is a passageway scoured through the cliff, by wave and river, through which the great rollers of the Indian Ocean sweep with thunderous force. The

Port St Johns, largest of the Wild Coast's resort centres, is named for the Portuguese galleon Sao João, *which foundered in 1552 with the loss of 100 lives. Its 440 battered survivors, including men of noble rank, set off northwards on a 1,600-kilometre (994 miles) overland journey that was plagued by setbacks, just eight Portuguese and 17 slaves eventually reaching the island of Mozambique, near present-day Maputo.*

Nelson Mandela

A young Nelson Mandela in traditional garb. His father was a chief of the Thembu royal house.

local Xhosa know the feature as *esiKhaleni*, which means 'the place of noise'. Its flat-topped, green-mantled summit is long and broad enough to accommodate several football pitches.

Make your way over the grassy hills of both the Ciskei and Transkei and you'll see a style of life that belongs to an Africa of another time. Here, like everywhere else in the country, the old ways are giving ground before the Western cultural onslaught, but much that is traditional survives in the country areas. The typical Xhosa homestead, or kraal, is a small cluster of rondavel-type huts, most of them built with their doors facing east. According to custom, the land itself is owned not by individuals but by the community; survival is a collective effort; everything is shared, in bad times as well as good, and Xhosa families still routinely help one another with such tasks as home-building and the tilling of the soil.

The Xhosa people are segmented into a number of major clans, each with its own customs, history and distinct cultural identity, and each divided into smaller groupings. The latter are led by an Inkosi (chief), who owes his position to the status of his mother even though Xhosa society as a whole functions along patriarchal lines. In day-to-day village life the women look after the home and the needs of the family, the land and its crops; the men customarily fulfil the roles of stockman, hunter and warrior, though the last two capacities have little relevance in modern times.

The Xhosa are of Nguni stock, and the body of their belief and lore has much in common with those of the Zulu of the eastern regions (*see* page 132). Basic to conviction is recognition of a Supreme Being, of the presence and power of the ancestral spirits, and of the *animus* of such apparently non-sentient things as rivers, rocks and trees. Here too, as in Zululand, spirit mediums play a prominent role in maintaining links with the ancestors, in foretelling, and in healing. A less fundamental and more visible element of traditional society is the variety and splendour of customary costume. The Xhosa were (and to a degree still are) known for their beadwork; clothing and ornamentation reflect the stages in a woman's life; one kind of headdress is worn by the newly married, another by a young mother who has given birth to her first child, and so on.

Right: A Xhosa homestead in the Transkei region. Although the land is overstocked and overcrowded, it remains a beautiful part of the country.

East London's harbour was slow to develop: the estuary is not naturally suited to accommodate large vessels and it was not until 1937, with the completion of the turning basin, that passengers could disembark directly onto the quayside rather than, as the practice had been, climb into baskets to be lowered onto lighters. Not too long afterwards the harbour was the focus of another, more noteworthy technical breakthrough: in 1961 its engineer invented an interlocking concrete breakwater block, known as a dolos *(the Afrikaans name for a knucklebone), which is now integral to harbour construction throughout the world.*

Cities and Towns

In area, the Eastern Cape is the second largest of South Africa's nine provinces: it extends across a little over 170,000 square kilometres (65,640 square miles) of remarkably diverse terrain that includes, in the north, the bone-dry plains of the Great Karoo and the high mountain ranges of the Sneeuberg, Winterberge, Stormberg and southern Drakensberg. To the south the countryside is gentler, kinder in climate and generous in its bounty, embracing the fertile soils of the Langkloof and the Sundays River Valley and a coastline of marvellous scenic variety.

It is also one of the poorer provinces. The majority of its seven million people are reliant in one way or another on a land that, in many places, is over-exploited and degraded. The region has very few mineral resources; development has been slow and patchy; unemployment remains at a high level, and many of the menfolk are forced to seek work away from home, in Cape Town far to the west and in the northern industrial centres of the Witwatersrand. Large-scale migrant labour has had a serious, even devastating effect on family life and on social stability.

Bisho, capital of the one-time Ciskei republic, is the seat of the provincial government, a modest little centre boasting handsome legislative buildings, an airport (which enjoyed international status at one time but was grossly underused), a business and shopping centre and a sprawl of high-density housing. But there is something contrived, artificial, about the town: it was deliberately created and developed, during the racially restrictive apartheid years, to accommodate the tens of thousands of black workers who commuted daily to the next-door 'white' industrial hubs of East London and King William's Town.

Much of the eastern region's economic activity takes place in and around East London, sited at the mouth of the Buffalo River and South Africa's only major river port. It was originally known as Port Rex but renamed (in 1848) when the area was annexed to the Cape Colony, and for a decade or so it served as the colonial headquarters of the distant 'border' area, the last frontier of white settlement. For years the place remained a rather neglected backwater, though it received some stimulus with the arrival, in 1858, of more than 3,000 German immigrants. Most of the latter were veterans of the Crimean War, tough legionnaires who found little of comfort in the remote outpost (life became a lot brighter when, later that year, 153 young women were imported from Ireland). Many of them made their way into the hinterland to establish farms, and to baptize their tiny hamlets – Stutterheim, Berlin and Hamburg among others – in memory of their European origins.

East London is now a substantial place, and a quietish holiday destination that offers fine beaches, pleasant parks and gardens and an equable climate: it enjoys an average of 7.5 hours of daily sunshine throughout the year. The wider municipal area is known as Buffalo City.

Rather special is the local aquarium (small, but the inmates are well chosen and displayed) and its museum, which houses the first coelacanth to have been caught in modern times. This primitive, mauve-blue fish – its scientific name is *Latimeria chalumnae* – flourished in the southern seas during the Mesozoic era and was believed to have become extinct 60 million years ago – until a specimen was landed near East London in 1938. Since then more of these living fossils have since been brought up in fishermen's nets. The museum also keeps the world's only known egg of the dodo, a large, ground-living bird that once thrived on the Indian Ocean islands until hungry seafarers hunted it to extinction. The last dodo died in Mauritius around 1680, though related species survived on adjacent islands until the 1790s.

Greater Port Elizabeth (officially the Nelson Mandela Metropole) is on the shores of Algoa Bay. By far the Eastern Cape's largest urban concentration, it was born in 1820, when 4,000 British immigrants made their landfall on the bay's gently sloping beaches. In the years that followed the town grew steadily, its wealth drawn from the prosperous (and, with the progressive defeat and dispossession of the Xhosa, increasingly peaceful) farmlands of the interior. The port served as the principal outlet for the region's beef, butter, grain and, most especially, for the wool and meat of the merino sheep. By 1861, when it achieved full municipal status, its population numbered a little less than 10,000; a fine Commercial Hall had made its appearance, and the thoroughfares were graced by elegant colonial residences, their architectural style reflecting the settlers' rural British origins. Some of the past has survived the decades, and is visible in the Regency-type townhouses on Cora Terrace, in the early Victorian balustrades and verandahs along Donkin Street and elsewhere, and in the gracious villas around St George's Park.

Greater Port Elizabeth is South Africa's fifth largest conurbation and a major port (fourth busiest after Durban, Cape Town and Richards Bay), the economic heart of the Eastern Cape and centre of an expanding regional tourism sector. Ford established the country's first motor assembly plant here, in the mid-1920s – it employed 70 workers, who managed to turn out 12 Model Ts a day – and the industry still serves as the city's industrial base. Unsurprisingly, this place is known as the 'Detroit of South Africa', though many of its 1,000-plus factories are unrelated to the motor trade. Its harbour encompasses some 3,500 metres (11,480 feet) of dockside, a container terminal, an enormous (10,000-square-metre; 107,640-square-feet) pre-cooling plant and mechanized ore-handling facilities, all of which are impressive enough but are barely sufficient to cope with the expanding maritime traffic. A brand new deep-water harbour, a little way east along the bay at Coega, is being built.

Port Elizabeth is also known by other names, among them the 'Windy City', although it is no more blustery here than anywhere else along the country's southern seaboard, and as the 'Friendly City', which is probably more apt. The place is not yet large enough to have become coldly impersonal, the local tourism authorities are both lively and competent, and they have a fair amount to offer. Principal drawcards within the city itself are four fine beaches – Humewood, with its next-door Happy Valley recreational area, is the most popular – and the museum complex. This latter is notable for its oceanarium: the resident dolphins, caught in the waters of Algoa Bay, are trained to play to the gallery, which they do with zest and humour twice a day in the enormous pool. Cape fur seals also take part in the act.

Not far from the city lies one of the country's more prominent wildlife havens. The Addo Elephant National Park, which covers a largish expanse of densely vegetated bush country 70 kilometres (45 miles) to the north-east, was created in the 1930s to rescue the last, sad remnants of the once great herds of Cape elephant. There was no room on the land for both the commercial farmer and these gentle giants of the veld, and it was the elephants that had to go:

The charismatic young Black Consciousness activist, Steve Biko, was perhaps the most compelling of martyrs to South Africa's struggle for freedom and justice. Born in King William's Town in 1946, Biko went on to found the South African Students Organization. He met a brutal death at the hands of Port Elizabeth security police in 1977.

STEVE BIKO

The Eastern Cape's magnificently varied coastline. TOP: Sunrise over one of East London's spacious beaches. The small coastal city is the country's only major river port. ABOVE: Farther up the seaboard, on the Transkei's well-named Wild Coast, is the Hole-in-the-Wall, a massive detached cliff through whose tunnel-like opening the surf thunders. RIGHT: Port Elizabeth, set on the shores of Algoa Bay and the Eastern Cape's largest centre. It is not, though, the provincial capital, a status held by the town of Bisho.

Port Elizabeth in the mid-1800s. The city began life as a reception centre for around 4,000 British immigrants brought in to settle the troubled 'frontier' region.

over the decades they were slaughtered to the brink of extinction. A few survivors – just 16 of them (later reduced to eleven) – managed to escape into the impenetrable tree-and-creeper tangle of the Addo bush, and there they were protected both by the inhospitable terrain and, coming almost too late on the scene, by an outraged public. Since then they have flourished: the local *spekboom* plant growth looks dismally unappetizing but these animals relish it, and the park now supports three times more elephants than any similar sized area elsewhere.

A short distance to the north, on the slopes of the grand Suurberg range, is the rather larger Zuurberg section of the Addo park, originally proclaimed to preserve the region's transitional vegetation (which comprises five major plant types) but destined to become one of the country's premier scenic and wildlife conservation areas. The landscapes, great tumbles of mountains cut through by deep river-valleys, are quite magnificent, their varied habitats home to a prolific number of different floral and bird species. Although much of the Zuurberg has been formally protected since 1896, its large-mammal populations suffered grievously from human depredation. The conservation people, though, are now bringing some of the animals – elephant, buffalo and rhino among them – back to their old home. There are imaginative moves towards creating

LEFT: Port Elizabeth's historic Town Hall fronts a spacious pedestrian plaza. ABOVE: A statue of Queen Victoria presides regally over The Friendly City.

Port Elizabeth was named by Sir Rufane Donkin, the Cape colonial governor of the time, in honour of his young, beautiful and recently deceased wife who, as an inscription in the city's Donkin reserve notes, was mourned 'by the husband whose heart is still wrung by undiminished grief'.

a 370,000-hectare Greater Addo park stretching from the Little Karoo south to the Indian Ocean, plus a 120,000-hectare offshore marine reserve.

The largest of the watercourses flowing through the Zuurberg is the Sundays River, which rises in the Sneeuberg and flows south-eastwards for 370 kilometres (230 miles) before discharging into the ocean at Algoa Bay north of Port Elizabeth. Its broad valley, enriched by deep, good alluvial soils, is wonderfully productive, especially in its middle reaches, yielding vast quantities of citrus (about half the national harvest) and fruit grown for their juices. A summer's day spent wandering up its course, when the trees are in bloom and the countryside is clothed in bougainvillea and frangipani, is delight indeed.

The coasts to either side of Port Elizabeth rank among the country's major holiday playgrounds. To the west is St Francis Bay, a wide sweep of sandy shoreline dotted by resort villages, of which Jeffreys Bay is the biggest. The latter is renowned for superb surfing rollers – the products of huge swells created by winter low-pressure systems – that challenge local surfers and international competitors alike. The beaches here are littered with lovely seashells, remains of both tropical Indo-Pacific and temperate marine species, and they attract collectors from afar. A fair selection of them, fashioned into ornaments, are on display in the town's museum.

Settler Country

The British settlers who stepped ashore at Algoa Bay in 1820 had high hope in their hearts, but disillusion soon enough set in. They were for the most part simple folk who belonged to what was known as the lower middle classes, people desperate to escape the grim economic depression of the era following the end of the Napoleonic wars in Europe. Of the 90,000 people who applied to join the immigration scheme, just 4,000 were chosen. They embarked, from London,

The Van Staden's River, to the west of Port Elizabeth, is reached via a spectacular pass which crosses its gorge along a 350-metre-long (1,148 feet) bridge built a dizzy 125 metres (410 feet) above the water, and the views that unfold are quite breathtaking. The nearby wildflower sanctuary conserves a lovely area of Cape chestnuts, cabbage trees, yellowwoods, white pears and massed plantings of proteas, watsonias, ericas and orchids.

OPPOSITE PAGE: One of the giant residents of Addo Elephant National Park. Its ancestors, persecuted to the edge of extinction, sought and gained sanctuary in what was described as 'a hunter's hell'.

Southampton and other port cities, in buoyant mood, determined to build better lives for their families in the brave new world of Britain's most recently acquired colonial possession.

The immigrants arrived in blissful ignorance of the realities – of the Xhosa presence in and their rights to the territory, and of the colonial government's true intentions. Warning bells sounded clear enough, though, when one party took leave of Jacob Cuyler, their guide, to make their way to their allotted farms, the nearest of which lay deep in the wilderness a week's journey away from the future Port Elizabeth. 'Gentlemen,' Cuyler said, 'when you go out to plough, never leave your guns at home.' It then dawned on them that they were to serve not only as farmers, but also as a kind of plain-clothes militia, the sinews of a 'living buffer' the authorities aimed to create between white settlement and Xhosa country.

One poignant recollection, penned by a certain Thomas Butler towards the end of the first season, illuminates their sense of disappointment and loss. 'My wheat,' he wrote, 'two months ago the most promising I ever saw in any country, is now cut down in heaps for burning .... The rust has utterly destroyed it. My barley, from the drought and a grub which attack the blade, produced little more than I sowed. My Indian corn, very much injured by the caterpillar; cabbages destroyed by the lice; the beans all scorched by the hot wind.... Our cows are all dry from want of grass; not the least appearance of verdure as far as the eye can reach. Nothing but one great wilderness of faded grass.'

The land had been taken away from the Xhosa, and it was exacting its revenge. For five years the settlers struggled against bitter odds. Many had been townsmen with little or no experience of farming, and certainly none in such bleak spaces. Their allotments were too small. There were locusts, floods, droughts, confrontations with the tribesmen, and an official ban on black labour. Many of them simply gave up and drifted into the small urban centres, most of which had started life as military garrisons. Eventually, though, around the mid-1820s, matters improved with the creation of larger farming units, a relaxation of government restrictions and, above all, the beginnings of what was to become a flourishing sheep-farming industry.

Of the white 'frontier' settlements, Grahamstown was the largest and most prosperous, capital of the new Albany district and headquarters of the region's military. It had had its share of troubles: in 1819 a 10,000-strong Xhosa army, led by Ndlambe and the prophet Makhanda (a nickname that referred to his left-handedness; his real name was Nxele), had attacked its stockades though the defenders managed, just, to hold out. Three years later the Xhosa again invaded the region, driving settler families in from the outlying areas. Many remained in town, bringing vital skills with them. Thereafter it developed, both commercially and politically, so that by 1831 the town was an important trading centre and could claim to be the Eastern Cape's principal settlement. Indeed, three decades later it became, for a brief period, the seat of the Cape government when the legislative assembly convened in the old military hospital (this was an attempt to placate those restless spirits who were lobbying for independence).

Today Grahamstown is an elegant place girded by green hills, its past discernible in the original, solid 'frontier' homes that have been preserved around Artificers' Square, and in the rather more imposing later 19th-century buildings erected in its more prosperous years. Predictably, it

The writer Thomas Pringle, one of the British settlers' leaders, noted his impressions of the promised land from the deck of the sailing ship Brilliant, *recording the 'sublimely stern aspect of a country so different from the rich tameness of ordinary English scenery'. The Scottish passengers, he went on, were especially affected 'as recollections of their native land were vividly called up by the rugged peaks and shaggy declivities of this wild coast. Some were excited to extravagant spirits; others silently shed tears'.*

A view of early Cradock by Thomas Baines. Like so many other Eastern Cape towns, Cradock began life as a military garrison in the bitterly disputed frontier region.

is informally known as the 'Settler City' and also, because of its theological college and its many churches, as the 'City of Saints'. The most prominent place of worship is the Anglican cathedral of St Mary and St George, whose bells, rood screen and lectern hold special interest, and whose spire rises above a piazza flanked on its south side by graceful Victorian facades.

Grahamstown is also an academic centre, home to Rhodes University and several fine schools, and to the 1820 Settlers Foundation, established to preserve Britain's cultural legacy. On Gunfire Hill, which overlooks the town, stands the Settlers' Memorial, a modern complex of auditorium, conference centre, exhibition halls, function rooms and entertainment areas. The monument is the nerve centre of the National Arts Festival, a showpiece of the country's (and, increasingly, of Africa's) creative talent. Here, each winter, drama is staged, music played, dances performed, paintings, sculptures and crafts displayed and entertainment offered. It is a vibrant, colourful occasion, and an important one for a continent struggling to find its identity.

The area's other smaller centres also have immigrant associations, ties that go back to the earliest days of colonial conquest. A short distance to the west, on the road to Grahamstown, is the village of Bathurst, a pretty little place nestling among the pineapple plantations, its precincts embowered by wild figs and coral trees. The town's two-pulpit church served as a fortified sanctuary during the 19th century; its Pig & Whistle Pub, which began life in 1821 as a blacksmith's forge, still plays amiable host to travellers. Some of the surviving early houses in Salem, to the west, are thick-walled, double-storeyed structures designed for defence, as was its Wesleyan chapel. A plaque on a nearby hill commemorates the courage of one Richard Gush, a Quaker whose soft words turned away a Xhosa war party. Salem, like most of the region's villages, is still discernibly English in mood; cricket has been played on its green since 1844.

OPPOSITE PAGE: The well-named Valley of Desolation, on the southern limits of the Great Karoo. Its peaks overlook the dignified old town of Graaff-Reinet. BELOW: A resident of the Mountain Zebra National Park, near Cradock.

Those small centres to the north of Grahamstown – Fort Beaufort, Adelaide, Somerset East, Bedford, Cradock and others – claim similar origins. Cradock, the northernmost, is not in fact part of what is regarded as traditional settler country although it, too, started out as a military outpost. It was founded in 1813 in the valley of the Fish River, 260 kilometres (162 miles) from Port Elizabeth and on the southern fringes of the Great Karoo though the valley, with its orchards and pastures and fields of bright green lucerne, is quite unlike the Karoo proper. The town has several claims to modest notability: its ilex oak trees, planted in 1850, are thought to be the largest of their kind in the world; one of its cottages, now restored, was for a while home to the celebrated writer and feminist Olive Schreiner, who wrote her best-known novel, *The Story of an African Farm*, while working as a governess in the area; and just outside town are the invitingly curative Karoo sulphur springs.

A little farther afield, just to the south-west, is the Mountain Zebra National Park, a wildlife sanctuary that hugs a great amphitheatre of the Bankberg range and was established to preserve the region's few remaining Cape mountain zebra. This animal is distinctively different from the more familiar plains or Burchell's zebra: it is smaller, and marked with an unusual transverse 'grid-iron' pattern of narrow stripes across the rump. The subspecies once ranged widely over the uplands of the Cape but by the 1930s had been reduced to just 25 individuals. The conservation effort proved highly successful, and today some 200 of the animals graze on the hillsides of the park. Many others have been translocated to reserves elsewhere.

To the west, and quite unlike Cradock in its origins and character, is Graaff-Reinet, 'capital' of the Karoo and one of South Africa's oldest towns. It was founded by Dutch-speaking settlers in 1786, folk who, a decade later, were independent enough of mind to drive out the local magistrate, declare a republic and install their own burgher government. This lasted for 17 months before they were forced back into the colonial fold, but the residents continued to defy British authority, determinedly and sometimes (in 1799 and 1801) aggressively. But the place settled down, matured with surprising elegance and eventually came to be known as the 'Little Athens' of the region. Unlike so many other South African centres that have developed haphazardly over the years, Graaff-Reinet was laid out, and its buildings designed and erected, according to a well-conceived plan. Today more than 200 of its structures, finest of which are Reinet House (now a museum) and the Drostdy (early magistrate's court and residence) are proclaimed historic monuments. Nearby is the 16,000-hectare (39,545-acre) Karoo Nature Reserve, set aside to protect the local succulent and Karoo scrub vegetation. Within its bounds is a remarkable fantasia of wind-eroded peaks, columns and rocks known, aptly, as the Valley of Desolation.

Chapter Eight

Northern Cape

The Great Spaces Washed with Sun

One bright morning in 1872 a slightly built youth named Cecil Rhodes, newly arrived on the diamond fields, watched the feverish activity of a vast concourse of dusty, sweating men crowded into a crater, a chasm gouged from the summit of a fabulously rich kimberlite 'pipe'. What he saw fired his imagination, and his ambition.

Rhodes's decision to stay, to make his fortune from the diamond-laden soil of Kimberley, was to have a profound influence on southern Africa. At that time the place was a sprawling, unkempt patchwork of tents, corrugated iron shacks, a few solid brick buildings and some 50,000 residents – a rather larger population than that of Cape Town, the colonial capital far to the south. Yet it was only six short years since the northern Cape's first diamond had been found.

In 1866 a young Korana boy picked up a shiny pebble on the south bank of the Gariep River near Hopetown and showed it to a Schalk van Niekerk, a neighbouring farmer. Van Niekerk eventually sent it – in an unsealed envelope – to Dr William Atherstone, a noted Grahamstown medical pioneer (among other things, he founded the country's first research laboratory) and an amateur mineralogist who, with the help of a local jeweller, identified the stone as 'a veritable diamond [which] weighs 21 and a quarter carats and is worth £500. Where it came from there must be lots more'. It was christened the Eureka, and its discovery caused quite a sensation in mining circles, but the prospectors who converged on the Hopetown area found little to encourage them and they soon abandoned the search.

Three years later, however, a Griqua shepherd named Booi unearthed another treasure, a magnificent 82.5 carat diamond which he sold to that same Van Niekerk (who in the interim had clearly learnt something about comparative values) for what he no doubt considered a fine price: 10 oxen, a horse and 500 sheep. In due course this stone, which came to be known as 'The Star of South Africa', found its way to England to be bought by the Earl of Dudley for £25,000, a huge sum in those days. Diggers flocked to the area to stake their claims – altogether about 10,000 plots were pegged – around Hopetown.

The main camp was at Klipdrift, close to a ford over the broad waters of the Vaal River, a once-peaceful crossing place used by generations of Tswana and semi-nomadic Khoikhoi on their way to and from their hunting grounds. Now, though, the tranquillity was gone, shattered by an unruly throng of men who fought among themselves, with the local chieftains and, soon enough, even with the Transvaal and Orange Free State governments for possession of a territory whose ownership had never been formally established. At one point, the culminating one in a turbulent and generally sorry saga, the diggers banded together to form their own Klipdrift Republic, a comic-opera affair that saw the election of a renegade named Stafford Parker as 'president'. The rebellion was short-lived, and Klipdrift was eventually renamed Barkly West. Today the river diggings are still a magnet for old-style fossickers, panhandlers who work the gravels and descend on the little town each Saturday morning to bargain with the diamond buyers.

OPPOSITE PAGE: The enchantment of Namaqualand. Springtime and the promise of warmth bring a bright colour to the plains. PREVIOUS PAGES: A scene in the Northern Cape interior, painted by the French traveller, François le Vaillant (1753-1824). The scene is entitled 'Claas Baster's Camp'. PREVIOUS PAGES INSET: One of the Kgalagadi Transfrontier Park's famed black-maned lions.

But all this was something of a sideshow to the real drama. Far bigger and more enduring deposits had been identified beneath the dry scrubland some 30 kilometres (20 miles) to the south. The most promising of several kimberlite pipes discovered in 1871 was that on a farm owned by the brothers De Beer: in July of that year a prospecting group known as the Red Cap Party began excavating a 10-metre-high (33 feet) hill – the famed Colesberg Kopje – and found that it contained diamonds in great quantity and of exceptional quality. The hill was soon levelled by the picks and shovels to become the beginnings of Kimberley's Big Hole.

The encampment grew overnight into a vast, unhygienic shanty settlement. Fortune-hunters came from many parts of the world and all walks of life: miners, traders, canteen-owners, teachers and parsons, adventurers, dealers legal and illegal, con-artists, gamblers, ladies of pleasure and other fringe people. The wealth extracted from the 'yellow ground', or surface kimberlite, was without parallel in the story of mining and money flowed like the proverbial champagne. Tents gave way to corrugated iron and mud-brick; hotels, bars, brothels, stores, churches, a school, a stock exchange and the renowned Kimberley Club made their appearance.

By the time Cecil Rhodes came onto the scene, just a year later, more than 3,500 claims had been registered, all of them small, most subdivided into even tinier plots, and upwards of 30,000 diggers were working cheek by jowl in the crater. Safety and efficiency were low on their list of priorities: as the hole grew deeper they constructed an immense cat's-cradle of aerial ropeways and the jumble of claims, walkways and steps became even more chaotic.

Scenes of early Kimberley. The original mine, or 'pipe', known as the Big Hole, yielded three tons of diamonds. ABOVE: the 'Big Box', more than 300 metres (1,000 feet) underground in the Kimberley Mine. RIGHT: At the diamond sorting tables. OPPOSITE PAGE: Locals pose for the camera outside a draper's shop.

Syndicates and companies were in fact evolving, but in 1885 the diggings were still divided into a patchwork of nearly a hundred separate blocks. Rhodes, now one of the major players on the local stage, decided to consolidate the fields and began buying up the De Beers claims (the enterprise had been named after the original landowners) and by 1887 he had become the sole owner of the company. Two years later, after a titanic battle of wills with Barney Barnato, the ebullient Jewish Londoner, he purchased the latter's even richer Kimberley Mine for a record £5,338,650. The cheque was framed and still hangs in the Kimberley Club. And then, with the later acquisition of neighbouring mines, Rhodes's De Beers extended its control over virtually the entire diamond industry.

Rhodes went on to make another fortune on the newly discovered Witwatersrand goldfields (though a far lesser one, largely because he failed to recognize the potential: a rare misjudgment), to become prime minister of the Cape Colony, and to carve out a brand-new country for himself across the Limpopo River.

Throughout his later years, though, Rhodes remained closely associated with Kimberley, principally because it was the focus, the fountainhead, of his financial empire but also for sentimental reasons. He was in residence there in November 1899, shortly after the outbreak of the Anglo-Boer War; found himself besieged with the rest of the populace when a Boer army cut the town off from the outside world for three long months, and drove the garrison commander to distraction with his constant meddling. He complained bitterly about the conditions, but he

In February 1900, during the siege of Kimberley, Theresa Stevenson wrote to her sister Louisa that 'the worst is standing waiting for your meat turn in the mornings. You stand two by two on the market square and the first morning Netta and I stood for more than 3 hours before our turn came. Then if you don't take your horsemeat, you get a soup ticket ... Louie, we are like skeletons here – over 200 children have died in the last two months. I am thinner now than after the typhoid fever, and Jack is just a frame.'

CECIL JOHN RHODES

lived well enough. Not so lucky were the ordinary citizens and, especially, the black labourers: rations were pitifully meagre; 1,500 whites and an uncounted number of Africans died, mostly of typhoid fever; infant mortality soared

The Big Hole continued to yield its glittering bounty until 1914, when the mine was finally closed down. By that time it had reached a depth of about 400 metres (1,300 feet), with another 900 metres of underground workings, and a circumference of about two kilometres (almost a mile), which made it the world's largest man-made crater. During its 43-year lifespan 25 million tons of the kimberlite ore body had been removed to produce 14,504,375 carats, or rather more than three tons, of diamonds.

Today the Hole, defunct and partly filled with water, forms the centrepiece of Kimberley's mine museum, an evocative array of buildings and relics that provides an insight into the city's lively past. Much of it is a re-creation of the early town: the cobbled Victorian street is lined by

period shops and cottages, a diggers' pub, a steam-train coach (used by the De Beers directors), Barney Barnato's boxing academy and other intriguing reminders of the town's salad days. Nearby is the old mine headgear and the De Beers hall, among whose exhibits is the Eureka diamond and the world's largest (616-carat) uncut stone. Other drawcards include Transport Hall (historic conveyances), and the museum's art gallery, which portrays Kimberley during its rumbustious infancy and adolescence.

Some 30 kilometres (20 miles) to the south of the city is Magersfontein, site of one of the Anglo-Boer War's costliest battles. Here, during the British 'Black Week' of December 1899, the burgher forces of the gifted Koos de la Rey stopped Lord Methuen's army in its tracks, pouring murderous Mauser fire into the advancing British ranks from a network of trenches. At the time this was a fairly novel defensive technique, but it was to be refined and used with devastating effect, 15 years later, in the killing fields of Flanders.

Aerial ropeways criss-cross Kimberley's Big Hole. At times the giant crater accommodated up to 30,000 diggers; conditions were chaotic until Rhodes began consolidating the claims.

The Land and Its People

Modern Kimberley is an unpretentious, medium-sized African city set in a dry, flattish, scenically unremarkable grassland and scrub countryside that supports cattle ranches and extensive irrigated farmlands. Four of the diamond pipes are still highly productive and several other minerals (iron, gypsum and salt among them) are mined in the area. Kimberley is also the principal urban centre in and capital of the Northern Cape, by far the largest and most sparsely populated of South Africa's nine provincial divisions.

The Northern Cape's boundaries encompass a little over 362,000 square kilometres (140,160 square miles) of the west-central and western parts of the country, an immense expanse of mostly sandy, semi-arid terrain that is home to just 850,000 people, or two for each of its square kilometres. About three-quarters of the population live in towns, chief of which – apart from Kimberley – are Upington in the far north; Kuruman, original headquarters of the London Missionary Society (to which David Livingstone, the great 19th-century explorer, belonged) in the north-east; Springbok in the far west; the railway centre of De Aar, and a number of fairly substantial sheep-farming centres.

This is also among the least developed of the provinces, its rains ungenerous, its infrastructure relatively undeveloped, its economic output accounting for just 2.0 percent of the nation's gross domestic product. Nevertheless it has its riches, most notably the diamond fields of Griqualand West and those around and to the south of the Gariep River mouth (*see* page 177); huge iron-ore deposits in the Sishen area to the south-east of Kuruman; the copper of the western coastal strip; manganese, fluorspar, marble and semi-precious stones.

Despite the generally poor soils and dry climate, too, the land is surprisingly bountiful, sustaining great flocks of sheep and, around Upington, a thriving karakul industry. Karakul sheep were originally introduced, from the Bukhara area east of the Caspian Sea, into neighbouring Namibia (then German South-West Africa) in

Diamonds have not provided the province's only mineral wealth. The presence of copper in the western regions had long been suspected (Cape governor Simon van der Stel personally set out in search of Namaqualand's fabled Copper Mountain in 1685). It was only during the 19th century, however, that serious copper-mining began – at Springbok and, later (1862) in the remote Okiep area. These hardy Okiep men, photographed circa 1890, are about to go underground.

The timeless reaches of the Gariep River. ABOVE: François le Vaillant's fanciful view of the 'Island of Hippopotamuses'. OPPOSITE PAGE: A twilight view of the Gariep ('Great') River.

1907 and made their appearance across the territorial border some ten years later. The combined region is now one of the world's biggest producers of both the pelts of the young (better known as Persian lamb) and the wool of the mature sheep.

The most rewarding source of agricultural wealth, though, is the Gariep River itself, which bisects the province on its 2,250-kilometre (1,400-mile) journey from its headwaters in the highlands of Lesotho far to the east. This is South Africa's largest watercourse, draining fully 47 percent of the country, and for almost its entire length it runs through the dry, treeless plains of the great central plateau. Its waters are erratic, the flow dictated by seasonal rainfall.

Almost the only greenery one sees over much of the countryside through which the Gariep passes are the thin strips of vegetation along its banks and, increasingly, the farmlands it irrigates. Indeed, large patches of the Northern Cape, as well as the soil-rich islands embraced by the river, have been transformed into lush oases of fruit orchards, fields of wheat, peanuts, maize and cotton, plantations of dates, and vineyards that yield grapes, raisins and sultanas.

The Gariep River's islands, of which there are many, have an especially colourful history. In the 19th century, some of them served as suitably remote and defendable hideaways for bands of rustlers, brigands and notorious 'river pirates'. These adventurous folk belonged to the Korana group, a semi-nomadic section of the Khoikhoi people who originally occupied the territory along the middle reaches of the Gariep. Other Korana filtered south, some as far as the southern coastal regions, but trekked north again in the latter part of the 17th century to escape Dutch settler authority. In the 1860s Korana raids provoked two colonial punitive expeditions, the second of which was directed against the river's densely wooded island refuges. The third and final 'war' was fought in 1877 and, although all three confrontations were inconclusive, the Korana eventually retired north towards the Kalahari.

The Korana have not survived as an entirely coherent cultural entity. Nor have the other long-time 'Coloured' residents of the Northern Cape region, the Nama (Khoikhoi) of the west and the Griquas. The latter have a complicated history: a people of mostly Dutch, Khoikhoi and,

When the summer rains are good the Gariep River becomes a swift-flowing torrent that sweeps across the land in a 8-kilometre-wide (5 miles) swathe; at other times it is benign, even sluggish.

AN UNKNOWN NAMA WOMAN

to a lesser degree, slave stock, they took their name from the Chaira-Griqua herders of the south-west, migrating away from the early white settlement, initially towards the Gariep River and eventually to what was to become Griqualand West – the region that contained Kimberley and its diamonds. In due course they were embraced by William Anderson's London Missionary Society (LMS), whose station at Klaarwater became known as Griquatown and the centre of an area described in the early 19th century as 'a republic under the patriarchal government of the missionaries'. This unofficial status was formally recognized in 1813, when the Griqua state received a written constitution, a president and council, and the right to mint its own coinage.

Today, the majority of the Northern Cape's Griquas, together with those many other inhabitants of Khoikhoi origin, are urbanized, and nearly all are Afrikaans-speaking. This is in fact the home language of 65 percent of the province's population, though English is being used more and more in formal communication. The other major language is Setswana, spoken by the region's 200,000 or so Tswana, a people related to the eastern Sotho and whose identity, in pre-colonial times, found expression through their numerous independent chieftains (*see* page 51). The traditions of those living in the northern regions of the country have largely disappeared, though the heritage remains remarkably intact in neighbouring Botswana, where they form the dominant ethnic group.

THE THIRSTLANDS

Most of the Northern Cape province is covered by the sandy soils of the Great Karoo, a vast semi-desert that stretches from the mountains of the southern coastal belt to and beyond the Gariep River. Much of the terrain is flat, featureless, the monotony here and there relieved by ridges and outcrops, rocky features pushed up through the shale and sandstone strata by aeons-old volcanic action and then weathered to jagged starkness by wind and periodic flood.

This is a region of heat and silence, and of immense distances; of roads that run as straight as arrows to the far horizons and seem to lead nowhere; of the occasional lonely farmstead girded by its windmill and by the green of willow and gumtree, a brave splash of colour in the monochromatic bleakness; of clear blue skies and bone-dry air, intense sunshine, scorching summer days and starlit, bitter winter nights. Very little draws the eye of the traveller passing through. But, still, there is something magical about the great, empty interior, a quality that seduces the senses, lifts the spirit, and lives in the memory long after the journey is done.

The name Great Karoo derives from the Khoikhoi word for 'thirst', and is apt enough: its better watered eastern parts are blessed with a modest 370 or so millimetres (15 inches) of rain a year; those in the bone-dry west receive, on average, less than a paltry 50 millimetres (2 inches).

At first sight the Karoo's vegetation is unremarkable, the ground patchily mantled by sparse grasses, scrub and low-growing shrubs that rarely merit a second glance. But look closer and you will see how superbly the plants – the aloes and crassulas, the euphorbias, mesembryanthemums and other succulents – have evolved and adapted to their harsh environment, surviving by the grace of roots and leaves that are able to store moisture. And, for a few days each year, the wilderness does have its floral beauty: when the rains fall the seeds of the wild desert flowers, dormant during the long months of drought, suddenly germinate to bring brief but exquisite colour to the landscapes. For all its surface dryness, though, much of the Great Karoo is well enough endowed with water. Moisture lies beneath the ground, and is drawn up by thousands of wind-pumped boreholes that, together with the scanty but sweet grasses of the eastern regions, nurture a high proportion of the country's nearly 30 million head of sheep.

In other parts of South Africa more and more opportunities are being offered the small farmer – the previously disadvantaged black man squeezed out by market forces, by the economies of scale and by the greed of the whites. The Karoo is different; its poor soils and low rainfall limit the land's carrying capacity, and only large farms are viable. The typical spread is enormous, owned by a farmer who has been born to and cherishes the great sunlit spaces.

The towns of the Karoo are few in number and far from each other. The most prominent of them – Beaufort West and Graaff-Reinet (*see* pages 213 and 156) – lie outside the Northern Cape's provincial borders, in the Western and Eastern Cape respectively. The others are barely more than ambitious villages, sleepy little places dominated by a high-steepled, white-painted, often surprisingly imposing church. Most are located in the eastern Karoo. The western parts are a lot more arid, emptier, desolate. This is the land of the *vloers* or pans, depressions scooped from the surface of the undulating wastelands. The massive, shallow basins fill with water during the rare rains and then dry out beneath the blistering sun to leave a residue of mineral salts, a whitish sediment that reflects the light with blinding brightness, disturbing the air above to create shimmering mirages and eddies of dust devils that rise and swirl across the flat land. Grootvloer, largest of the pans, measures some 60 by 35 kilometres (37.5 by 20 miles); the most well-known is Verneukpan, whose name means 'deception', a reference to its mirages.

The Karoo farmer is probably Afrikaans-speaking, of independent mind, reticent and courteous. And his hospitality is legendary: his forebears settled this formidable land and survived their isolation because they were tough and resilient people, secure in their large families and their Calvinist faith, but also because they had a wider sense of community, and they welcomed passing strangers because that was the way news was exchanged, goods bought and sold, and loneliness relieved.

A desert storm sweeps across the plains of the Kalahari. Although termed a desert, the region is home to a surprising variety of plants and animals.

Sands of the Kalahari

The Northern Cape's second largest town is Upington, located on the Gariep River, hub of the vast and largely empty Gordonia magisterial district and a major communications centre (the rail bridge across the river is an impressive 1,067 metres, or 3,500 feet, in length; the local airport has the southern hemisphere's longest runway). Despite its semi-desert setting it is an attractive place, girded around by the lushness of irrigated farmlands. A short distance downriver is Kanoneiland, a spacious island thickly wooded in parts, intensively cultivated in others.

Travel even farther along the river, to a point 120 kilometres (75 miles) west of Upington and you will see one of southern Africa's more striking natural features. Here the mighty Gariep River narrows and courses turbulently through the Augrabies Gorge, an immense, steep-sided ravine flanked by towering granite cliffs weathered to starkness by wind and river. A broad expanse of the adjacent, rather bleak countryside has been set aside as a national park, originally established to protect the area's rugged landscapes, unusual rock formations and modest complement of wildlife, and later extended to serve as asylum for, among other species, the endangered black rhino. This part of the province is an ideal haven for these primeval mammals: remote, sparsely populated, and relatively safe from poachers.

Opposite: The porous Kalahari soils retain no surface water; rains are rare, sporadic and unpredictable. But when they do come, they turn the arid, sun-scorched countryside into verdant parkland. Below: A cheetah, swiftest of all land animals, patrols the dry reaches of an ancient riverbed.

The handsome gemsbok is superbly adapted to desert life: it does not need water (the animal gets its moisture from tsamma melons and other plants), and has evolved a highly efficient temperature control mechanism.

North of the Gariep River the terrain, its soil and plant life undergo subtle but clearly discernible changes. This is the southern extremity of the Kalahari Basin, a vast (2.5 million square kilometre, or nearly one million square mile) region that covers the whole of Botswana, the eastern areas of Namibia and parts of Zimbabwe, Angola and the Democratic Republic of Congo (formerly Zaïre), as well as a small segment of South Africa.

The Kalahari is termed a desert, and technically it might be because its sandy, porous soils cannot retain water. But the countryside is probably better described as wilderness, for its broad plains are mantled by grasses that, though scanty and ephemeral and wholly dependent on meagre and patchy rainfall, sustain multitudes of game animals. Only in the far south does the land resemble the popular perception of a desert: here there are high red dunes, some of them

clad in straggly coats of tough grass and broom, and 'rivers' that remain dust-dry for most of the time. The two most prominent of these watercourses are the Auob, which flows on average every ten years or so, and the Nossob, whose reaches run with water once in a century. Nevertheless the soils of the riverbeds nurture a surprising profusion of trees: handsome camelthorns, blackthorns, shade-giving shepherd's trees and other kinds of acacia.

But for the most part the animals of the desert, certainly the bigger herbivores, draw most of their sustenance from the perennial plants of the open country, patches of grassland fed by the rare and unpredictable rains and feeding, in turn, the nomadic and sometimes multitudinous herds of blue wildebeest, stately eland, high-stepping red hartebeest, graceful springbok and scimitar-horned gemsbok. Preying upon these is an array of carnivores that includes the distinctively black-maned lion, the leopard, the cheetah and, that supreme opportunist, the spotted hyaena.

A pair of black-backed jackals in quarrelsome mood. These versatile creatures – they will eat just about anything that moves and much that doesn't – are remarkably brave, often nipping at the heels of hyaenas and lions to gain access to a carcass.

This is a hostile land. Water is at a premium, food is never plentiful, the summer heat is intense (70°C; 160°F at ground level), winter night-time temperatures plunge well below zero – and the fight for existence is ferocious and never-ending. But the living forms of the desert are adapted to its harshness, and although the plants wither in the long droughts and individual animals die of starvation, sometimes in appalling numbers, there are enough survivors at the coming of the rains to ensure the future, to create new generations.

Part of the South African portion of the region – a stretch of sandy plain and dune country wedged between the borders of Botswana and Namibia – has been protected within the Kalahari Gemsbok National Park, established in 1931 to stop the indiscriminate slaughter of the antelope herds. The effort has, by and large, proved highly successful despite the erection of game fences on three sides. Along the Nossob River, which forms the common border between South Africa and Botswana, there are no artificial barriers and the game is free to follow the ancient migratory routes, which the herds do in sometimes spectacular fashion. And they do so in relative safety, for a vast chunk of territory on the Botswana side is also a proclaimed conservation area. The two segments were recently combined to form the vast Kgalagadi Transfrontier Park, the first of southern Africa's cross-border or 'peace' parks (*see* also page 95).

The southern Kalahari was until recently the last refuge of the Bushman (also known as San) in South Africa (*see* page 17). Today the various clans, groups which once roamed without hindrance, have abandoned the nomadic lifestyle in favour of a more settled existence, most of them outside the park. Some, however, have remained within its borders, where they work as rangers and as uncannily skilled trackers. They are highly respected for their intimate knowledge of the ways of the wilderness. And there are moves, tentative ones at the time of writing, to return the remainder of these displaced people to their ancient hunting and gathering grounds.

West to the Atlantic

After passing through the Augrabies gorge the Gariep River negotiates its last, desolate stretch through northern Namaqualand to empty into the Atlantic Ocean. The countryside around and to the south of its estuary is sandveld, barren-looking, a semi-desert that supports scattered communities of Nama folk and whites of settler, mostly Afrikaans-speaking stock. Copper mining provides a living for some; most of the others depend in one way or another on the unforgiving land. On and beneath the sandy soils, however, and in the offshore waters, lies immense wealth.

Over the ages the Gariep (and other now long-gone rivers) brought countless diamonds, leached from the surface kimberlite and gravel beds of the interior, downriver to the sea, where they were scattered by tidal action and the currents. Many were then swept ashore, onto the coastal sands. With the passing of the Ice Ages the ocean level fell, later rising again but not to its previous mark, so that what was once shoreline now forms, in places along the west coast, dry marine terraces or 'raised beaches'. It is on these, and especially in the area around the remote seaside towns of Port Nolloth and Alexander Bay, that the best gemstones are found.

Although the presence of diamonds in the region had long been suspected (in fact they were being mined north of the Gariep River mouth, in today's Namibia, before 1910), the first gemstone was discovered south of the estuary only in 1925. In some parts the business of locating the treasure was simplicity itself. It lay everywhere, on or just beneath the ground, and it was made even simpler by a curious physical phenomenon: the diamonds occurred in places that also contained fossils of a now-extinct type of warm-water oyster. The two elements – gemstone and shellfish – have nothing in common, but both were affected at some time by a geological upheaval that altered the ocean's currents, killing the oysters and bringing the diamonds ashore. The diggers profitably used this 'oyster line' as a beacon to the wealth of the ancient gravels.

Port Nolloth and Alexander Bay are the centres of what became the state diamond diggings, but northern Namaqualand's principal town is Springbok, inland and astride the main highway that runs 1,500 kilometres (932 miles) from Cape Town north to Namibia's capital, Windhoek. Springbok itself is of little note, though it does have a rugged outback kind of charm and, nearby, the fairly extensive Goegap Nature Reserve, a place of huge, dome-like granite outcrops and sandveld that sustains a plant life technically known as Namaqualand Broken Veld Vegetation. The springtime displays, within the reserve and in the surrounding countryside, are quite beautiful. This floral wealth has its rivals elsewhere: indeed, for a few brief weeks in spring almost the whole of Namaqualand is covered by glorious carpets of wild flowers (*see* page 222).

Far to the north, within a broad loop of the Gariep River, lies the Richtersveld National Park, a product of long negotiation between government and the local herders. The protagonists agreed to establish a 'contractual' park that would safeguard the land for all the interested parties – the stock-farmers, the tourists, the naturalists, the plants and the wildlife. The experiment has proved a success, much to the delight of the environmentalists, for in botanical terms the Richtersveld is very special, home to the unique *halfmens* tree, and to fully a third of all known species of mesembryanthemum. It is also memorable for its landscapes, for the wind-sculpted rock pillars and spires of the northern parts, and the desolation of its southern scrubland plains.

OPPOSITE PAGE: Perhaps the most sociable of all the Kalahari's animals is the endearing meerkat, or suricate. Groups habitually appoint a sentry to watch out for predators while the others forage for food.

The promise of wealth close to Alexander Bay was fulfilled when Dr Hans Merensky, a geologist and leading figure in the charting of the fields, picked up 487 diamonds from beneath one flat rock and, during the single month of September 1926, collected a total of 2,762 more.

ABOVE: 'Augrabies' is a Korana word for 'big waters', an appropriate name for the Augrabies Falls, whose cataracts cascade over the rim of the great canyon. The Augrabies complex is ranked among the world's six largest waterfalls.
RIGHT: Horses roam through Namaqualand's sandveld.
OVERLEAF: A solitary quiver tree in the vast and lonely spaces of the Richtersveld. Hostile though the terrain appears, it nurtures half of all known species of mesembryanthemum.

Chapter Nine

Western Cape

The Province of Good Hope

Table Mountain, arguably the southern hemisphere's best-known landmark, towers more than a kilometre above the buildings of central Cape Town, its straight-edge summit flanked by the twin buttresses of Devil's Peak and Lion's Head. On a clear day this distinctive and awe-inspiring threesome can be discerned from ships more than a hundred kilometres (62 miles) out to sea.

Those who make their way to the top of Table Mountain, either by cable-car or on foot, are treated to wondrous vistas – of Cape Town's streets and embowered squares below; of the harbour and its ships; of the Twelve Apostles, a line of sentinel-like peaks that guard the western seaboard; of Robben Island, once prison home to Nelson Mandela; of the broad sweep of False Bay to the east and the distant Hottentots-Holland range rising blue-grey above the coastal plain. Running away to the south is the Cape Peninsula, a narrow finger of land whose mountainous spine ends in the massive cliffs of Cape Point.

All too often, though, the views are obscured by what is known as the 'tablecloth', billows of misty vapour that tumble down the mountain's precipitous northern face. At these times the soaring heights take on a sinister, almost menacing personality, their 'sable cloud, which in darkness shroud' said to hide the spirit of the immortal giant Adamaster, defeated in a war of rebellion against the Grecian god Jupiter and banished to the Cape. Other legends of the mountain are less classical, the product of local imagination and perhaps of experience as well. For instance there's Antje Somers, a malevolent little bogeyman who, dressed as a woman, waylays and robs those who stray from the path, leaving them naked on the windblown slopes. Antje was probably a real person at one time, and grandmothers still conjure his presence to frighten small children. More fanciful is Jan Hunks, an old Dutch pirate who challenged the devil to a tobacco-smoking contest, so creating the clouds.

Probably the best time to make the ascent is in the early evening, when the last of the sun can be caught and the lights of the city are beginning to appear far below. At the top are viewing points, a restaurant, a shop (from where you can send faxes, and post letters and postcards bearing the Table Mountain postmark) and a number of short walks through the summit's nature reserve, which sustains an extraordinary profusion of indigenous flora.

Table Mountain's slopes and its well-watered central plateau are home to most of the Peninsula's 2,600 or so different kinds of plant. These in turn belong to a botanical region, known as the Cape Floral Kingdom, that extends over the winter-rainfall areas of the country's southern and south-western parts and which, although it accounts for a minuscule 0.04 percent of the earth's land surface, is so richly endowed that it enjoys peer status with the great Boreal Kingdom embracing North America and most of Europe and Asia. The plant life here, collectively called *fynbos* ('fine bush'), is quite remarkable in its variety: it comprises more than 8,600 species (compared with 15,000 for the whole of Australia), the majority of them hardy,

OPPOSITE PAGE: Table Mountain rises above the waters of Table Bay, an unmistakable landmark for generations of seafarers. PREVIOUS PAGES: Ships at anchor in Table Bay in the early age of steam. The painting, by Thomas Baines, is dated 1847. PREVIOUS PAGES INSET: A dainty Cape sugarbird on its protea perch.

JAN SMUTS

Jan Christiaan Smuts (1870-1950), the greatest statesman of the country's pre-democratic era, retained an abiding love for Table Mountain, and continued to walk its slopes until late in his long life. Smuts's place in 20th century history – as soldier and political leader – is well documented. However, he was also a philosopher of note (his Holism and Evolution *drew critical acclaim), and he ranked among the major botanists of his time. His special study was the grasses of his native country.*

low-growing, evergreen shrubs that are well adapted to the long summer droughts, and which flourish in (for the most part) nutrient-poor soils in environments ranging from sub-alpine mountainsides to coastal sands. Fully 6,000 of them are unique to a specific and limited area, some of them to micro-habitats. As many as 120 different species have been found growing in a single patch the size of a suburban back garden.

Many of the plants are quite lovely when they flower, among them the orchids, the disas, the red-hot pokers, the heathers (or ericas, of which there are more than 600 kinds) and, especially, the proteas. The latter, named after Proteus, the Greek god who could change his shape at will, include the pincushions, with their beautifully coloured flowerheads; the sugarbush; the creamy white blushing bride; the rare and dainty marsh rose, and the king protea, South Africa's national flower. Largest of the family is the silver tree, which grows to a height of 10 metres (33 feet), whose green leaves have an enchanting silvery sheen when they quiver in the Cape breezes. All of this – the Mountain, its extension to Cape Point and much of the flanking metropole area – falls within the recently proclaimed Table Mountain National Park.

PLACES FROM THE PAST

Cape Town is the country's oldest city, site of its parliament and capital of the Western Cape, one of South Africa's richer provinces. It huddles in the natural amphitheatre formed by Table Mountain, the flanking buttresses and Table Bay. Its southern suburbs – some of which started life in the 1650s – gird the mountain's slopes and extend along the line of rail that leads to Simon's Town, not far from Cape Point. The rugged western seaboard, dominated by the stark immensity of the Apostles, remains (for the time being) relatively undeveloped. To the east and north are the Cape Flats, a low-lying sandy plain that once, not too long ago on the geophysical calendar, lay beneath the ocean but which is now covered by suburbs and informal settlements. Beyond the Flats are the lovely hills and valleys of the Cape winelands and, farther out, the southern extremity of the Great Karoo. The provincial boundaries encompass two entirely different stretches of coast, one running northwards into a region of desolate sandveld, the other eastwards across the green luxuriance of the country's southern marginal zone.

By international standards Cape Town is a small city – its central area, confined by sea and mountain, runs to little more than twenty blocks – but it has personality, a character very much its own, animated, cosmopolitan, self-assured, confident enough of its maturity, skills and resources to have made a serious bid for the new millennium's inaugural Olympic Games. It was founded by the first Dutch settlers, matured slowly and with considerable style, and the legacy of its graceful past is to be seen everywhere. At the top of Adderley Street, the main thoroughfare, are the public gardens, laid out more than three centuries ago as a vegetable patch and now an oasis of greenery where, even though you're just a stone's throw from heavy city traffic, you can commune with the quieter muses. The Gardens hold more than 8,000 different kinds of local and (mostly) exotic plants, tall and beautiful trees, a network of shady pathways, a modest scatter of statuary, an aviary and a pleasant tearoom. Fringing the area are some grand buildings, among them the Houses of Parliament, the National Gallery (the nearby memorial to Jan Smuts, white South Africa's foremost statesman, is worth more than a passing glance), the Great and Old synagogues, the South African Museum and its planetarium, and the South African National Library, a handsome edifice modelled on the FitzWilliam Museum in Cambridge, England.

Long Street, once the lively commercial heart of Cape Town, is now rather run-down, lined with junk shops, fast-food outlets and the like, but a fair number of its late-Victorian buildings have survived the passage of the years, delightfully filigreed relics of the wrought-iron age whose facades are gradually being restored to their original, charming condition. And here and there amid the concrete and glass of the central area and in the leafier suburbs you'll come across places that date back to much earlier and more stately times, elegant mansions with lofty ceilings, huge teak doors, green-shuttered windows, shady verandahs and secluded courtyards decorated by vines. Perhaps the city's finest example of traditional Cape domestic architecture is Koopmans-De Wet House on Strand Street, originally built in 1701, enlarged several times and now a period museum displaying a splendid collection of local and European furniture.

Cape Town's oldest still-occupied building is the massive, five-sided, stone-walled Castle of Good Hope, completed in 1679 and designed to guard the fledgling Dutch settlement from invasion from the sea. It later served as the military, administrative and social hub of the Cape Colony. The imposing entrance is noted for its clock tower whose bell, cast in 1697, is still rung on special occasions; bisecting the spacious, open interior courtyard is a defensive cross-wall, known as 'De Kat', that once held cannon but is now graced by a rococo balustraded balcony that overlooks the governor's residence and grand reception hall (now a museum).

A view of Cape Town's Grand Parade, with the Castle of Good Hope in the background, during the early years of the 19th century.

Perching on the slopes of Signal Hill, just to the west of the city centre, is a dense cluster of little flat-roofed houses that were built in the late 18th and early 19th centuries. The streets are narrow; here and there you'll see a minareted mosque, and hear the muezzin calling the faithful to prayer. This is the so-called Malay Quarter, more correctly known as Bo-Kaap (literally, 'above Cape'), home to part of the region's large Islamic community.

Many Cape Muslim families are descended from slaves brought in by the Dutch colonists during the early years, people who over the decades contributed enormously to the development of the region and were finally released from their bondage in the

1830s. The first of the Muslims to arrive, though, was Sheik Yusuf, by no means a slave but, rather, a revered spiritual leader and high-born prince who was both related to the king of Goa and, it was said, a direct descendant of the Prophet Mohammed himself. Yusuf had led an insurrection against the Dutch in Java, fighting a bitter, years-long campaign against the self-proclaimed overlords, but was eventually forced to capitulate. In 1693 he was exiled to the Cape as a 'political prisoner', and on his death six years later was laid to rest at Fauré, east of Cape Town. His *kramat*, or tomb, is regarded by the region's Islamic society as one of its holiest shrines.

The Bo-Kaap's houses have survived the predations of the developers (it is a proclaimed national monument) and the area is undergoing a slow facelift, the buildings gradually donning fresh coats of plaster and paint. Other less fortunate parts of historic Cape Town, however, have vanished in their entirety, some of them beneath what is known as the Foreshore. Until quite recently this 145-hectare (358-acre) segment of the city, just to the north of the central area, lay beneath the ocean: it made its appearance during dock construction in the 1930s and 1940s, when massive quantities of dredged sand were dumped on the leeward side of the old harbour. The fishermen's beach, together with the leisure area, the seafront palms and the splendid old pier, was replaced by a wasteland of grimy quaysides, dockyard buildings, tank farms, security barriers and a great raised highway that cut Capetonians off from their beloved harbour.

Sir Donald Currie's Castle (later Union Castle) steamship line, remembered with affection by thousands of British immigrants, began vying for the lucrative South African mail and passenger trade in 1872. Pictured is an early on-board programme of events from the steamer *Dunottar Castle*. The last mailship, *Windsor Castle*, sailed out of Table Bay on 6 September 1977.

But during the past few years some of the colour and vitality has returned: city and sea have again been united by the imaginative and highly successful Victoria & Alfred Waterfront redevelopment scheme, a multi-million-rand enterprise that has drawn inspiration from harbour rejuvenation projects in Sydney, Boston, San Francisco, Vancouver and other parts of the world. The Waterfront, though, is not merely imitative: it has been created to meet Cape Town's special needs; it has its own distinctive character, its unparalleled setting beneath the moody grandeur of Table Mountain, and it is both impressive and unique.

The Victoria and Alfred basins, the oldest part of the harbour and consigned to redundancy when the new docks were completed, have been transformed into a brilliantly animated tourist playground that now rivals the mountain as Cape Town's premier drawcard. Many of the early dockside structures have been converted and new ones built to serve as hotels, restaurants, pubs, umbrella-shaded bistros, cinemas (including the giant IMAX, the world's largest screen format), museums, theatres, craft and produce markets, speciality shops, a wine centre, a brewery, the fine Two Oceans Aquarium and much else. The overall design embraces open quaysides, promenades, piazzas and a yacht basin. Moreover, this is not just a fun place: it continues to function as a worked-in, lived-in area; tugs and salt-stained fishing boats use the basins; the graving dock still operates; offices are open for business; apartment complexes are making their appearance.

Yesterday and today. The old Victoria & Alfred dockland area (opposite page, bottom) has been replaced by Cape Town's glamorous new Waterfront development (below).

The reclamation of the sea brought its commercial rewards, but it also destroyed forever what local author Lawrence Green remembered as 'the liveliest corner of the waterfront .... A beach of oars, tackle boxes and snoek kerries, anchor ropes and stone anchors. It was a memorable sight when the whole fleet put to sea under spitsails and jibs and the scene on their return was even more vivid. For then, all the old Malay priests and grey-bearded hadjis in Cape Town, all the bright-skirted Malay womenfolk and fezzed small boys seemed to be waiting on the sand. Then the fish carts were piled high and the fish-horns sounded triumphantly ...'.

Wealth and Poverty

For more than three centuries Cape Town relied for its prominence and prosperity on its position astride the maritime trading routes, and on its harbour. This is still very much a port city. The docklands are now a lot quieter than they were in the heyday of the passenger liner, when Union Castle mailships vied with each other for the ocean speed records: Durban and Richards Bay in the east, which are closer to South Africa's industrial heartland, have siphoned off much of the seagoing traffic. Nevertheless, the harbour remains the country's second biggest. Major elements of the local economy include marine fishing and fish processing (Cape Town is the headquarters of South Africa's commercial fleet), light engineering, high-tech manufacture, printing and packaging, banking and insurance, export fruit and wine.

And tourism. The region is fast becoming a major destination for the world's travellers: the mountain; the Waterfront; the lovely beaches; the vineyards, orchards and scenic beauty of the hinterland; the lively calendar of arts; the myriad eating and drinking places; the rather laid-back, undemanding pattern of life, all combine to create a highly attractive basket of enticements.

That is one face of the city. It shows a metropolis of fine buildings, graceful thoroughfares and an ambience that has more of Europe about it than of Africa. This Cape Town welcomes visitors with a smile, entertains them royally and sends them away replete with pleasant memories.

But there is another, darker side. Across the sand-blown Cape Flats to the east are vast, densely packed townships and 'informal settlements' of small, box-like homes, rudimentary shacks and shelters thrown together with cardboard and plastic sheeting. The poverty and deprivation are massive. Greater Cape Town, the metropolitan area that stretches from the village of Kommetjie near Cape Point to Atlantis in the north, has a population of about 3 million, a figure that is rising by the year. Most of the newcomers are black families from the 'traditional homelands' of Ciskei and Transkei far to the east (*see* page 141), regions that are plagued by overcrowding, soil erosion and a grievous shortage of skills and investment capital.

The past has compounded their problems. Under apartheid, the Western Cape was classified a 'Coloured preference area', which meant that opportunities in the labour market were reserved for Coloured applicants. Blacks were forbidden jobs, prohibited from settling in the region and thousands were forcibly removed. The policy was, of course, unworkable as well as morally repugnant: most black families escaped the dragnet; others – those who were translocated – simply made their way back. But since they were considered 'illegal' very little was done to develop the townships. The influx has created an urgent need for more houses, schools, clinics and other services. The financial burden is heavy, the social consequences tragic, the solutions distant.

Others also suffered enormous disruption through the operation of the apartheid laws, and most notably that of the Group Areas Act. The people of the Bo-Kaap (*see* page 187) belong to a much wider Cape society of both Muslim and Christian faith. One of their traditional homes was District Six, a vibrant, close-packed inner suburb of rickety buildings and narrow lanes that was declared a 'white' area in 1966. Thereafter it was demolished, and its 55,000 residents moved to the brand-new, characterless town of Mitchell's Plain and to other places on the desolate Cape Flats. Just one or two structures – churches and mosques – escaped the bulldozers.

Writer Brian Barrow remembered District Six as a town 'of rusted roofs, turrets, minarets, towers, arches, ornate facades, colonnades and Gothic spires, dazzling in their variety and colour ... As one of the world's great meeting places of people of many races, religions and colours, it proved that none of these things matters'.

District Six before the removals. LEFT: A groom completes his wedding rituals at a mosque. BELOW: Children play in Upper Ashley Street.

There's an intriguing element of mystery, of fantasy and fable, about Cape Point, for it is here that the Flying Dutchman, the phantom ship with its broken masts and tattered sheets, is condemned to sail the southern seas till the end of time. The legend was born more than three centuries ago, when the Dutch captain Hendrik van der Decken, his storm-tossed vessel foundering, swore to round the Cape even if it took him until doomsday to do so. Providence accepted the challenge, and several 'sightings' have been recorded over the decades, most prominently that made by the future King George V while he was serving as a Royal Navy midshipman.

Officialdom claimed it was all part of a slum-clearance programme, and indeed District Six was a ramshackle, unsanitary and crime-ridden warren. But it had colour, vitality, personality and, especially, a powerful sense of community. Its streets were a pandemonium of people, cars, horse-drawn wagons, hawking carts; general dealers that stocked everything from dried beans to banjos, dimly lit little shops filled with spices and herbs and joss-sticks. It had a soul.

District Six, renamed Zonnebloem, was prime real-estate, but the developers kept away and most of it has remained a wasteland for three decades, a silent reminder of government at its most insensitive. Now, at last, it is being returned to the people, and one day it may, just possibly, regain something of its old magic.

Cape Point and False Bay

Popular belief has it that the eastern shores of the Peninsula are lapped by the warm waters of the Indian Ocean, the western ones by the chilly Atlantic. In reality the separation, the technical demarcation, occurs off far-away Cape Agulhas (*see* page 206), Africa's southern extremity. Nevertheless, stand atop Cape Point and the interaction of two great ocean currents can actually be seen. And there are other differences: sea temperatures are a lot higher, and the prevailing wind a lot stronger, in the east than in the west.

Cape Point is one of the region's finest viewsites. Take the funicular railway up to the viewpoint at the base of the old lighthouse and look over the blue immensity, and you'll capture images that will linger in the mind. The cliffs fall sheer to the ocean far below, where dolphins, seals, sometimes whales can be seen; gulls and gannets wheel in the sky above; to the north and east the shore runs in a wide golden arc to the hazy heights of Hangklip.

The Point falls within the Cape of Good Hope Nature Reserve, a sanctuary noted more for its floral wealth than its wildlife. A full 1,200 different indigenous plant species have been identified on the ridge that flanks the eastern shore, and in springtime the display is breathtaking. But it does have its animals, among them mountain zebras, springbok, eland and other antelope, the caracal (a largish cat), Cape foxes – and chacma baboons. These last, a troop of which frequents the Point's parking lot, are thought to be unique within the primate world in their taste for marine foods, which they garner from the seashore at low tide. They are also used to begging for and receiving handouts and are familiar, indeed often over-familiar, with visitors.

False Bay is so named because early mariners, bound for Table Bay, sometimes mistook Cape Point for Cape Hangklip at the northern end – a costly and, in rough weather, all-too-often fatal error. Today the coastal strip plays a more benevolent role: it is a mecca for anglers, surfers, boating enthusiasts and sun-worshippers. The shoreline comprises a 35-kilometre (20-mile) stretch of continuous white sand punctuated by rocky patches and, along the southern section, a scatter of pleasant seaside towns and resort villages linked by the coastal road and by rail. Each has its character, its distinctive attractions. Muizenberg, a rather old-fashioned place much loved by the Victorian gentry, is famed for its wide, immensely long beach. 'White as the sands of Muizenberg, spun before the gale,' wrote Rudyard Kipling, who spent many a summer day here.

OPPOSITE PAGE: The Cape Peninsula ends, dramatically, in the great cliffs of Cape Point.

The Atlantic Seaboard

Standing out to sea, and clearly visible from the suburbs of Green Point and Sea Point, is Robben Island, once informally known as 'South Africa's Alcatraz' and notorious for its role as a maximum security area for political prisoners of the apartheid era. Nelson Mandela spent many of his 27 years' incarceration in one of its prison cells. So, too, did scores of other liberation activists.

But the island's history goes much further back. Portuguese, English and Dutch seafarers hunted marine mammals ('Robben' is Dutch for 'seals') and scavenged for seabird eggs along its rocky shores; the later Dutch colonists garnered its seashells (to produce lime) and quarried its 'beautifully veined' slate and stone. It was also used as a gigantic livestock pen. And, in 1654, Jan van Riebeeck, seeking to enlarge the infant settlement's depleted larder, introduced rabbits onto the island – a minor innovation but, so the story goes, one that was to have profound repercussions in a land far away. The fast-breeding leporids, of course, flourished on the good, carnivore-free pasturage, and when Captain Cook weighed anchor in Table Bay a century later the island was swarming with them. Cook took a few on to Australia and these, so far as is known, were ancestral to the great rabbit infestations that were to devastate that country's farmlands.

Over the years Robben Island also functioned variously as an internment camp for paupers, lunatics, the chronically sick and the unwanted – and as a penal colony. It hosted convicts as far back as the 1600s; inmates included political exiles from Holland's eastern possessions – among them the princes of Ternate and Madura, who are honoured in the island's *kramat*, or Muslim shrine – and the Xhosa prophet Nxele. The latter, who had waged a bitter war against the British in the eastern 'frontier' region, was captured in 1819, consigned to the island, led a mass escape and drowned when the fugitives' boat capsized in heavy seas.

These days, though, Robben Island has a different and kindlier purpose, serving as memorial to the liberation struggle, and as a nature sanctuary for Damara and Caspian terns, jackass penguins and some 30 other types of seabird. The prison has been preserved intact and this, together with the island's lovely arum lilies, its tiny village and turn-of-the-century church, its rugged coastline and the fine views it affords of Cape Town and Table Mountain, makes it both a place of pilgrimage and an increasingly popular tourist attraction.

But back to the mainland. From Sea Point the coastal route – Victoria Drive for much of the way – heads south, past the trendy beaches, upmarket apartments and expensive villas of Clifton and Camps Bay and then through virtually deserted, scenically splendid landscapes. To the left are the lofty, often mist-shrouded heights of the Twelve Apostles; on the right rocky coves and cliffs that tumble down to meet the Atlantic rollers. Eventually you'll get to the seaside village of Llandudno, hugged by the hills and as pretty as a postcard, and, just beyond, the bigger but in its own way just as attractive town of Hout Bay. 'Hout' is Afrikaans for 'wood', and it refers to the dense stands of yellowwoods and other hardwood trees that once mantled the steep mountain slopes that gird the place. The area is still beautifully wooded; the blue waters of the

Remembrance on Robben Island. OPPOSITE: Nelson Mandela, on a visit to his former cell, reflects on his long and painful walk to freedom. BELOW: Defiant Xhosa chiefs were imprisoned on the island during the 'frontier' wars of the mid-1800s.

LEFT: The Cape Peninsula's 'Riviera' – the seaside suburbs of Cape Town's Atlantic coast – ranks among the country's most fashionable residential strips. Superlative scenery and trendy beaches are its major assets. OVERLEAF: Portrait of proteas. The region's Floral Kingdom embraces some 370 different species of these plants. Enormously varied in form, they were named (in 1735, by the Swedish botanist Carl Linnaeus) after the mythological Greek god who could alter his shape at will. Clockwise from left: king protea; blackbearded protea; pincushion protea; *Protea aristata*; and yellow pincushion protea.

The stately homestead of Groot Constantia, south of Cape Town, was originally the home of Dutch governor Simon van der Stel, a man of enterprise and impeccable taste. The wine cellar's cherub-adorned pediment (above) is the work of the celebrated French-born sculptor, Anton Anreith.

bay, the harbour and its rows of bobbing leisure and working craft (snoek is the main catch) and the soaring Sentinel massif, complete the picturesque setting. After Hout Bay the coast road twists its way up and along the flank of Chapman's Peak in a 10-kilometre (6-mile) scenic drive that must rank among the world's most spectacular.

The inland route, that which makes its oak-lined way up the Hout Bay valley and down into the gladed parklands of Constantia, leads to the earliest and arguably the stateliest of the region's many historic mansions. Groot Constantia was designed, built and, from 1685, occupied by governor Simon van der Stel. A little less than a century later the estate was taken over by the Cloete family whose patriarch, Hendrik, had a gift for wine-making, and the sweet, rich, red Constantia vintages became famous, finding their way to the aristocratic and even royal tables of Europe (Napoleon featured among satisfied customers). Hendrik also had an eye for beauty, adding on a graceful two-storeyed wine cellar, the work of the noted French architect Louis Thibault. The elegant, beautifully thatched homestead, designed in the classic U-shape of the Cape Dutch idiom, is appropriately furnished in period style. An avenue of oaks leads from the house to an ornamental pool where the notables of early Cape Town disported themselves and where, according to startled eyewitnesses, the amiable ghost of Van der Stel sometimes appears.

In the same general area, but closer to the city, is Kirstenbosch, widely recognized as one of the world's great botanical gardens. Here around half of South Africa's 18,000 indigenous species of flowering plant are cultivated – proteas, ericas, pelargoniums, mesembryanthemums (known locally as 'vygies'), ferns, ancient cycads and many others. To visit the area, to walk along its many pathways on a fragrant spring day, is delight indeed.

THE CAPE WINELANDS

Beyond the Eerste River to the northeast of Cape Town lies the Boland, a region of many moods and faces, of grand mountain ranges, emerald valleys, gentle pastures, vineyards and orchards weighed down with fruit. It is a lovely part of the country, each season bringing its own enchantments: in high summer the air is hot and heavy with the scents of the harvest; in autumn the colours change to create a symphony of russets and golds, and slow-moving farm trucks bear great loads of sweet-smelling grapes to the pressing rooms. Snow covers the backing peaks in winter; springtime carpets the countryside with a profusion of wild flowers.

The majority of Cape Dutch buildings are thatched, thick-walled, white-washed. Many are graced by a prominent front gable, a feature that began simply as an upsweep of thatch to allow space for a loft-window but which grew larger and more decorative and, with time and steady refinement, became a thing of beauty.

This was the first of the rural areas to be colonized by the Dutch: they began infiltrating the lands of the indigenous peoples – the nomadic Bushmen (also known as San) and the Khoikhoi pastoralists – in the 1660s, turning the rich alluvial soils over to wheat, to pasture, and soon enough to the fruits of the vine. The farms flourished, white occupation of the countryside expanded and permanent settlements – hamlets of simple little houses clustered around a Protestant church – made their appearance.

And as the landowners prospered, so they spread themselves, extended their modest frontiersman homes, changed the roof-pitch to accommodate a gabled loft, added wings, slave quarters, stables, coach-houses, a *jonkershuis* (the house set aside for the family's eldest son), laid out

Most of the country's late-maturing export grapes are produced in the Hex River area north of Cape Town. The valley is a delight to the eye in any season, but especially so when summer greens turn to the muted shades of autumn and early winter.

courtyards, the whole farmyard (or *werf*) encircled by a wall to project a comfortable image of settled security. And by the end of the 17th century a distinct form of architecture had begun to evolve, a style that drew on the domestic traditions of a number of countries – of medieval Holland and Germany, the France of the Huguenots, Indonesia – but which developed over the decades in unique fashion to become known, and admired, as Cape Dutch.

Stellenbosch is the oldest of the country towns. It was founded in 1679 beneath the imposing heights of the Papegaaiberg ('parrot mountain') in the green and pleasant Eerste ('first') River valley, and grew gracefully in keeping with its setting. The early residents planted oak trees, created open spaces, erected some splendid homes and public buildings, and it has all been carefully preserved. Old Stellenbosch can be seen at its best along Dorp Street, which boasts the longest row of historic structures in the country. The town is also an important educational

Picking waterblommetjies – 'little water flowers' – near Paarl in the Cape winelands. These plants provide the basis of a piquant local dish.

centre, and has been so for something more than a century, home to prestigious schools and to a university that has served as Afrikanerdom's intellectual breeding ground. The minds of generations of white prime ministers, politicians, academics and business leaders were moulded in its culturally exclusive lecture halls and tutorial rooms, though since the mid-1990s it has had to come to terms with the new, non-elitist South Africa.

Other Boland towns also have their distinctions. Paarl is the largest: founded in 1720 as a farming and wagon-building centre, its main street runs for ten jacaranda-shaded kilometres (6 miles). Paarl is noted for the bounty and beauty of the surrounding countryside – the lush Berg River valley – and for its one-time prominence in the hard-fought, ultimately successful struggle to gain recognition of the Afrikaans language. It was the base from which many of the linguistic pioneers worked; on the slopes of the mountain is the Language Monument, a graceful structure of spire, fountain, and three linked columns. Each of the latter symbolizes a debt owed by Afrikaans – to Europe, to Africa, and to the slaves brought in from the East.

Franschhoek's name, and those of many of the area's dignified mansions, commemorates a far smaller but still significant cultural force. In 1688 the first tiny group of French Huguenots (Protestants), refugees from a Europe ravaged by war and religious persecution, settled in the exquisite Drakenstein valley, bringing some much-needed skills to the infant colony. But although (or perhaps because) they were independent of mind, isolationist even, officialdom deliberately mixed them in with the resident Dutch and German farmers, and within a few decades very little remained of their cultural heritage – French was no longer spoken, and assimilation was complete. They were, though, influential in the development of the wine industry, and of the elegantly evolving architecture of the period. Many common Afrikaans names are of Huguenot origin, among them Malan, Du Plessis, Le Roux, Marais, De Villiers and Du Preez.

Part of Franschhoek's Huguenot Memorial, which honours the small community of 17th-century French Protestant refugees who settled here. Their Gallic culture lives on in the names of the area's homesteads, and in those of many Afrikaner families.

Somerset West, near the coast to the south of Stellenbosch, is a largish and fairly attractive centre, unexceptional in itself but it does have two notable attractions. The Helderberg Nature Reserve, though modest in extent, is magnificent in its mountain setting and its plant and birdlife. Not too far away is Vergelegen, one of the oldest and grandest of the historic estates and a classic example of Cape Dutch architecture at its youthful best. It was built by the extravagent governor Willem Adriaan van der Stel in 1701, at enormous cost to the public purse (Dutch East India Company money, materials and slaves were used in its construction) and its orchards, orange groves and 18 cattle posts were a great deal larger and better founded than those of the average colonial freeburgher. Public outrage eventually forced Van der Stel from office in disgrace. The Vergelegen mansion and its thatched extension look much the same as the originals; the grounds are a delight, their centrepiece the Octagonal Garden, which embraces a wrought-iron and trellised ambulatory and more than 300 species of flowering plant. Especially splendid are the trees: they include camphors planted in 1700, a rare dawn redwood (once thought to be extinct) and a twisty old mulberry, sole survivor of an early 1700s silk-making experiment.

Through the northern parts of the Boland flows the Breede River, its valley one of the largest, loveliest and most productive in the region. Close to the headwaters is Ceres, an enchanting town named after the Roman goddess of agriculture and centre of a rich fruit-growing area that yields massive quantities of apples, pears, peaches, nectarines. Nearby Tulbagh, founded in 1743 and charmingly picturesque, suffered the country's worst recorded earthquake in 1969 (6.5 on the Richter scale), a local disaster that destroyed many of its – and the country's – finest old townhouses. But in the years that followed they were beautifully restored to their halcyon condition and those on Church Street – 32 in all – now comprise South Africa's largest single collection of historic buildings. Among the region's other centres are Worcester (the open-air museum is well worth a visit) and Robertson, in an area celebrated for its excellent brandies, sherries and jerepigos – sweet, heavy wines made from the rich, white muscat grapes.

The Boland is covered by a network of wine routes, itineraries modelled on the famous *routes de vin* of France and the German *Weinstrassen*. Stellenbosch's is the oldest and largest: it encompasses 22 private cellars and five co-operatives, all within a 12-kilometre (7.5-mile) radius of town. Others are almost as extensive, and between them they provide around 2,000 different wines. There can be few more pleasant ways of exploring this entrancing part of the country than to follow their leisurely courses. Many of the estates were laid out in the very early years, and the gabled homesteads, shade-dappled grounds and broad vineyards are lovely beyond measure.

The Gentle Land

The region to the east of the Hottentots-Holland range, which is breached by the dramatically scenic Sir Lowry's Pass, is known as the Overberg ('beyond the mountain'), a gentle land of prosperous wheat and barley farms, cattle spreads, forest plantations, and a coastline attractively endowed with cliff-girded bays, resort villages and tranquil seaside towns. The ocean, too, can be gentle, but is not always so: here, a great many ships have come to grief over the centuries. Some of their corpses can still be seen; but the majority are hidden beneath the shallow waters of the Agulhas bank. The most celebrated of the wrecks was probably that of the *Arniston*, a British troopship that went down in 1815 with the loss of 372 lives.

The tragedy occurred near Cape Agulhas, southernmost point on the African continent but, apart from that, quite modest in character. The Cape is simply the southern extremity of an inland plain that slips beneath the waves to become part of a wide (250-kilometre; 160-mile) segment of the continental shelf. The seas here are among the world's richest fishing grounds.

Largest of the Overberg's towns is Hermanus, pleasantly laid out between mountain and sea and a one-time fishing hamlet, whaling station and lime-making centre (the shore is rich in seashells). Later, sporting anglers, yachtsmen, holidaymakers and retirees joined the community and its character changed dramatically. Among other things it now boasts a modern marina complex, but the old harbour is still there, complete with its slipways and work-worn boats, serving as an open-air museum and a memorial to the tough fisherfolk of yesteryear. Hermanus overlooks the waters of Walker Bay, which attracts numbers of massive, oddly graceful southern right and other whales in wintertime, which is both the breeding and calving season for these marine giants. They can best be viewed from the shoreline cliffs above the town, their arrival heralded by the official 'whale crier'.

OPPOSITE PAGE: The beauty of an Edwardian summer's day near the Overberg town of Greyton.

Inland, well to the north of Hermanus, lies Swellendam, which was born in the 1740s in what was then the far frontier of colonial settlement. It lived peacefully and elegantly enough for the first half-century of its life – the beautiful drostdy (magistrate's court and residence) is the most impressive of its historic buildings – but then its delinquent burghers rose in rebellion against and declared their independence from the authorities in Cape Town. The Swellendam 'republic' lasted a bare three months.

In the hills of the Langeberg to the north of Swellendam is the extensive Marloth Nature Reserve, where black eagles can often be spotted wheeling and gliding among the peaks and ravines. To the south is another conservation area, one with an especially heart-warming story to

tell. By the 1830s the bontebok, a largish antelope of the plains, was very close to extinction, the herds shot out by generations of farmers and 'biltong-hunters' ('biltong' is sun-dried meat), but a small group of landowners had the foresight – remarkable in that generally unconcerned era – to keep the few survivors safely on their spreads. A century later the first Bontebok National Park was established, in the Bredasdorp area near Cape Agulhas, with just 17 of the animals in residence. The park was then moved, in the 1960s, to its present location and now supports a population of about 200. This is its maximum carrying capacity, but over the years surplus bontebok have been translocated to other reserves and the total, worldwide, stands at between 2,000 and 3,000 – a healthy enough number to assure the future of the species.

The good earth of the Overberg region yields splendid harvests of wheat, barley, fruit and much else.

PREVIOUS PAGES: The wonderland of water along the Garden Route. On the left are Langvlei (top) and Swartvlei (bottom), which form part of the Wilderness lake system. On the right is the lovely beach at Nature's Valley in the Tsitsikamma National Park.

NATURE'S ENCHANTING ABODE

Mossel Bay, on the seaboard 396 kilometres (246 miles) east of Cape Town, derives its name from the fat mussels savoured by the indigenous 'Strandloper' people who inhabited the area, on a seasonal basis, before the coming of the white man. It was also the landfall of the first Europeans in modern history to touch South African soil. Dias, Da Gama and other Portuguese seafarers called in for fresh water, and in 1501 João da Nova camped out on the shores, staying long enough to erect a small stone chapel in honour of his God and for the spiritual welfare of his crew (nothing remains of this, the country's earliest European-style building). The modern town's extensive museum complex celebrates these colonial pathfinders and the subsequent decades of exploration and settlement.

Today Mossel Bay is the hub of South Africa's nascent oil industry: modest offshore fossil-fuel deposits have been charted (at enormous and arguably unwarranted cost) and are being exploited to meet a little over 5 percent of the country's needs. It is also one of the centres along the famed Garden Route, a scenically spectacular segment of the southern maritime belt that stretches 250 or so kilometres (160 miles) to the Storms River mouth in the east.

The Garden Route is a cornucopia of visual delights. On one side are the densely forested, well-watered slopes of the Cape Fold Mountains – the Langeberg, Outeniqua and Tsitsikamma ranges – and on the other the blue Indian Ocean, its shores a pleasing succession of broad embayments and secluded coves, cliffs, tumbling rocks and pretty little river estuaries. Between the two is the 'garden' itself, a coastal terrace of green fields, wooded valleys, a profusion of wild flowers and clear, scented air, all of which prompted 18th-century French traveller François le Vaillant to observe that 'Nature has made an enchanted abode of this place'.

George is the biggest of the Garden Route's towns, a place of spacious oak-lined streets set in, to quote François le Vaillant, 'the most beautiful land in the universe. In the distance we spied the mountain range covered in proud forests. Below us lay the extensive valley, decorated by shapely hills alternating with countless undulating forms down to the sea ...'.

The highway eastwards takes in the village of Wilderness, its lagoon and five lakes – large and limpid sheets of water animated by great flocks of waders and other waterfowl – before entering the town of Knysna. Here, too, is a lagoon, 17 kilometres (10.5 miles) long, guarded at its sea entrance by two imposing bluffs known as 'The Heads' and a natural treasure-house that sustains an enormous variety of living forms – birds, fish, crabs, prawns, the rare seahorse *Hippocampus capensis*, oysters that find their way to the country's best restaurants, and a host of other aquatic species. Knysna itself is as attractive in its own unpretentious way: it is a largish town known for a range of appealing local products that includes cheeses, ham, honey, trout, oysters of course, fine furniture fashioned from the local hardwoods, and superb draught ale. All around are the deep-green swathes of the Knysna forest, which, when combined with the adjacent Tsitsikamma, forms the largest area of indigenous high forest left in South Africa, a 34,000-hectare (84,000-acre) home to stinkwoods, ironwoods, handsome yellowwoods (some of the giants grow to 50 metres and more in height, and are well over 1,000 years old), white alders, Knysna boxwoods, blackwoods and many others.

Part of the coastal plateau to the east of Plettenberg Bay has been set aside as the Tsitsikamma National Park, a proclaimed area that extends a short distance out to sea as a marine reserve. This is an exquisite stretch of countryside, which falls within the Eastern Cape province but is still part of the Garden Route. The park is richly endowed with ferns, proteas, ericas, aloes, wild orchids, a remarkable variety of lilies and with majestic stands of Cape chestnut trees, hardwoods and white milkwoods – a botanical diversity that attracts some 280 different types of bird. Among the more colourful of the latter are the paradise flycatcher and the turaco (formerly known as the Knysna loerie). Rivers and streams that rise high on the mountains run through the Tsitsikamma forests before discharging into the ocean; along the shoreline are inlets and embayments, golden sands and rock pools alive with a myriad marine creatures.

Beaufort West is a fairly substantial town of streets embowered by pear trees and home to a trio of fine buildings that, together, comprise the local museum complex; on display in one of the houses is memorabilia relating to heart-transplant pioneer Chris Barnard, who was born here and grew up in the area.

The Cape Karoo

North of the coastal mountains lies the Great Karoo (*see* page 170), some of whose southern sands lie within the Western Cape. Indeed the Karoo's principal urban centre is part of the province: Beaufort West straddles the main highway leading from Cape Town to Johannesburg, Pretoria and beyond into south-central Africa (this was the first section of Cecil Rhodes's dreamed-of Cape to Cairo route).

Matjiesfontein, just off the highway and much closer to Cape Town, comes as a delightful surprise to travellers driving through the monotonous Karoo landscapes. Victorian down to the last lamp-post, it was built in the 1880s – by one Jimmy Logan, an enterprising Scotsman with flair, good taste and a worrying chest complaint – as a dry-air health resort and soon attracted a fashionable clientele that included, among other notables, the writer Olive Schreiner (who was asthmatic), Cecil Rhodes, the British politician Lord Randolph Churchill (Winston's father) and the Sultan of Zanzibar. The local hotel, an elegant hostelry called The Lord Milner, regularly wins honours for quality and ambience.

Quite different in character is the Little Karoo, a distinctive and in parts scenically dramatic region that lies between two separate segments of the southern rampart. The plain, 250 kilometres (160 miles) long and 70 kilometres (45 miles) wide, is flanked in the south by the Outeniqua and Langeberg ranges, in the north by a spectacular chain of mountains known as the Swartberg. Here and there roads find their tortuous way up and over the heights and the vistas – of deep, vegetation-tangled ravines, of hillsides covered in wild flowers and, in the distance, the coastal terrace and the ocean – are memorable. The Little Karoo forms part of the same geological system as the Great Karoo but has little else in common with its big brother. Rainfall is low, yet plenty of water flows down from the uplands, bringing rich deposits of alluvial soil that nourish fine crops of wheat, grapes, tobacco and fields of emerald green lucerne.

Oudtshoorn, the region's principal town, is informally known as the 'feather capital' of the world, a name that derives from its central position in the ostrich-farming industry. During late-Victorian and Edwardian times these big birds were the mainstay of the local economy. European designers, caught up in the Art Nouveau movement and its emphasis on organic, flowing lines, fastened on feathers as the perfect fashion accessory, creating and embellishing hats, headbands, reticules, cloaks, fans and boas from the decorative plumes. During the boom London buyers willingly paid £100 for a pound of prime ostrich feathers – an astronomical price in those days – and the Little Karoo's farmers and traders suddenly found themselves immensely rich. The wealthiest of them, simple folk for the most part, rural and unsophisticated, took to the most ostentatious of lifestyles, building themselves hugely opulent, multi-roomed, marble-floored 'feather palaces' embellished with turrets and gables and wrought-iron trimmings. One or two of these architectural extravaganzas can still be seen in and around Oudtshoorn.

A few kilometres to the north of Oudtshoorn is a labyrinthine system of underground caverns that ranks as one of South Africa's more impressive natural wonders. These are the Cango Caves, once inhabited by prehistoric man, 'discovered' by a local farmer in 1780 and now a prime tourist attraction. Cango One, the first of the five known complexes to be opened up,

Linking the town of George to the Little Karoo is the Outeniqua Pass, built in the early 1940s with the help of Italian prisoners-of-war. Splendid views unfold along its entire 16-kilometre (10-mile) length.

comprises 28 chambers (they are linked by nearly three kilometres [2 miles] of passages) that are remarkable in the colours and shapes of their dripstone formations. Largest of them is the Grand Hall, 107 metres (350 feet) in diameter; Botha's Hall features a petrified and quite exquisite 'waterfall'; and nearby is a towering column called Cleopatra's Needle. And there are other modest marvels – the Rainbow Room; the Bridal Chamber, complete with its calcified four-poster bed; the Drum Room, which has a crystalline 'drum' that reverberates when struck; the 24-metre-long (77 feet), low-ceilinged corridor known as Lumbago Alley; and Lot's Chamber, with its human-like figures frozen in time.

Aloes decorate the foothills of the Swartberg Pass, whose summit towers 1,585 metres (4,755 feet) above sea level. The higher slopes are covered with proteas and watsonias in summer, with snow in winter.

The Cederberg is a botanist's delight, a floral wonderland decorated by a myriad endemics ranging from bright spring annuals to handsome indigenous forest trees. More than 70,000 hectares (173,000 acres) of the region have been proclaimed a controlled wilderness area, and it is a fine place for walking, camping and rock-climbing.

Mountains and Coast

The land to the north of Cape Town, that running up South Africa's western seaboard to the Olifants River, is scenically pleasant, in some places strikingly beautiful. Much of it is also immensely fertile. The area around Malmesbury, on the main inland highway, is known as the Swartland ('black country') for the dark, rich earth that sustains pastures and great golden swathes of wheat. Farther on, in the valley of the Olifants, there are more wheatfields but also vineyards, tobacco plantations, orchards of subtropical fruits and, above all, of citrus. The orange groves that mantle the hills around the little town of Citrusdal are the country's third largest but, because this is a frost-free winter rainfall region of sandy soils and long, hot summers, they probably surpass all in the quality of their fruit.

Nearby Clanwilliam functions as the headquarters of South Africa's rooibos tea industry: the needle-leafed shrub (*Aspalathus linearis*) grows wild in many parts of the Western Cape but is happiest on the slopes of the Cederberg range to the east of the Citrusdal-Clanwilliam axis, and this is the only area in which it is systematically cultivated. The plant has always been valued, by the local Nama people and by rural white families, for its multiplicity of medicinal properties: the aromatic beverage is certainly soothing, and there is good reason to believe it can also relieve such ailments as insomnia, stomach cramps, bronchitis, infant colic, nervous tension, various allergies and, when directly applied, nappy rash and other skin disorders. It contains no caffeine and hardly any tannin and, unsurprisingly in this health-conscious age, is in growing demand even beyond the country's borders.

The Cederberg is a magnificent stretch of highland terrain, a place of lofty peaks covered by snow in winter, weirdly weathered rock formations, clear and icy streams, waterfalls, pools and spellbinding vistas. The mountain range takes its name from the rare and once almost extinct Clanwilliam cedar, a tall and lovely tree that suffered grievously from the woodman's axe and from uncontrolled veld-burning (to improve livestock pasture) during the early years of white settlement. A few of the cedars, though, managed to survive in the higher places and these, now strictly protected, should ensure the future of the species. Another, even less frequently encountered plant is the pure-white snow protea, which clings precariously to life above the snow-line and occurs nowhere else on earth.

An alternative route north is along the coastal road, a pleasant drive along or near a shoreline that is scenically rather bare, even stark in its featureless simplicity, but in places remarkably attractive. It leads to Saldanha Bay, one of the country's finest natural harbours. The early navigators, and succeeding generations of European visitors, more or less ignored the place because the area is dry and drinking water scarce, but not too long ago it began to develop and is, today, a major centre of the West Coast fishing industry, a deep-sea terminal for the export of iron ore railed down from the northern interior (its harbour can accommodate the largest of bulk carriers) and site of a new, multi-billion-rand steelworks around which other industries are clustering.

All of which raises serious environmental issues. At Saldanha Bay's southern end is Langebaan Lagoon, a narrowish, 20-kilometre-long (12.5 miles) inlet and focal point of a superb but fragile wetland wilderness now enclosed within the West Coast National Park. The lagoon

This charming painting by François le Vaillant, of a homestead and camp on the Olifants River, evokes the simple life of the region's early white settlers.

and its surrounds are something of a paradise for bird-watchers: its clear, shallow waters, its tranquil salt marshes, the mud- and sandbanks that host countless crustaceans, marine algae, tiny snails and other nutritious organisms, attract an enormous concourse of aquatic birds to the area. Most of these visitors are migratory waders (notably curlew sandpipers) who leave their breeding grounds in the frozen wastes of Siberia for the long flight across Russia and the Middle East to their southern summer home. Other arrivals, among them the sanderlings and knots, make their way around the great bulge of West Africa. The rocky shores and islands of the bay itself, which are free of predators, offer roosts and nesting sites to upwards of a million seabirds. Indeed the entire West Coast is renowned for its birdlife (as well as for its crayfish catch). It is at its most

RIGHT: A soft sea-mist shrouds the salt-stained boats of Lambert's Bay, headquarters of the West Coast's fishing fleet. The bay, and indeed the whole of this coastal region, is renowned for its birdlife. ABOVE: Cape gannets on Bird Island, which lies within the harbour.

SILVER FISH ADF441KKB
SILVER FISH

visible, perhaps, at Lambert's Bay, largest of several charming little fishing centres whose small 'island' (it is in fact connected to the harbour wall) hosts more than 250 different avian species.

Farther north, beyond the Olifants River and into Namaqualand, the air becomes hotter, the countryside drier, less visually pleasing. This is an arid, bleak, sparsely populated region. Surface water is almost non-existent (though thick fogs, created by the interaction of cool Atlantic current and warm atmosphere, often roll in from the sea), and at first sight the land seems barren, incapable of supporting any but the hardiest, least visually appealing forms of life. Yet it sustains a vast profusion of succulents and flowering plants that, in spring, cover the plains and hills in glorious carpets of colour.

Altogether, the western sandveld is home to more than 4,000 different floral species, most belonging to the daisy and mesembryanthemum groups although others – such as aloes, lilies and perennial herbs – are well represented. The plants are drought-resistant, their seeds lying dormant during the long, dry months, but after the winter rains and before the coming of the drying desert breezes, when the earth is warming and the pollinators are abroad, they burst into brief and beautiful life. The floral displays are by no means confined to the Namaqualand region; they extend southwards to decorate the countryside around Cape Town and the Peninsula's eastern approaches.Especially lovely to behold are the springtime slopes of the Cederberg, the enchanting Biedouw Valley and, closer to the coast, the pleasant little town of Darling and its immediate surrounds.

Left: Sheep graze the modest pastures of the western coastal belt. In springtime, though, the land is mantled in a marvellous profusion of wild flowers. Overleaf: A few of the region's myriad floral species, including daisies (top left, bottom right), gazanias (top right) and vygies (bottom left).

Index

Page numbers in **bold** *refer to photographs.*

FRONT COVER: (TOP ROW) Port Elizabeth, Eastern Cape; Nelson Mandela in his cell on Robben Island; **(MIDDLE ROW)** Kruger Rands symbolic of the Witwatersrand's rich gold history, Gauteng; A male lion resting in the Kruger National Park, Mpumalanga; Tree silhouette at sunset on Signal Hill, Western Cape; **(BOTTOM ROW)** Cape Town's Atlantic Seaboard; Mat-makers near Makhado, Limpopo Province from a bygone era.
BACK COVER: The old Victoria & Alfred dockland area, Western Cape.
SPINE: Windmill at sunset, KwaZulu-Natal Midlands.
HALF TITLE PAGE: View towards Monk's Cowl and Cathkin Peak, KwaZulu-Natal.
TITLE PAGE: Fishing boats at Arniston (Waenhuiskrans), Western Cape.
IMPRINT PAGE: Street scene, Kimberley, c. 1876.
CONTENTS PAGE: Windmill and dam, Free State.